Arizona Politicians

Arizona Politicians

THE NOBLE AND THE NOTORIOUS

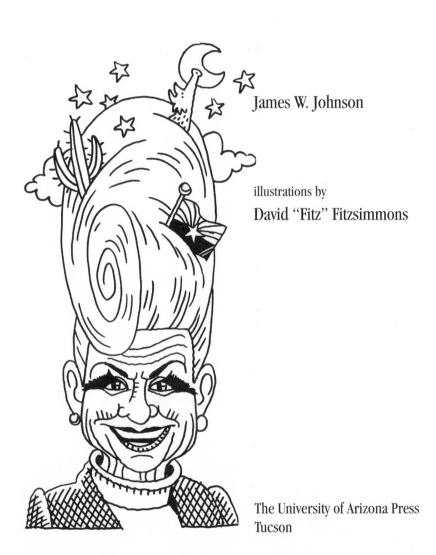

James W. Johnson

illustrations by
David "Fitz" Fitzsimmons

The University of Arizona Press
Tucson

The University of Arizona Press
© 2002 The Arizona Board of Regents
First Printing

⊗ This book is printed on acid-free, archival-quality paper.
Manufactured in the United States of America

07   06   05   04   03   02   6   5   4   3   2   1

Library of Congress Cataloging-in-Publication Data
Johnson, James W., 1938–
Arizona politicians : the noble and the notorious /
James W. Johnson ;
illustrations by David "Fitz" Fitzsimmons.
p. cm.
Includes bibliographical references and index.
ISBN 0-8165-2202-2 (cloth : alk. paper)
ISBN 0-8165-2203-0 (pbk. : alk. paper)
1. Politicians—Arizona—Biography. 2. Arizona—Biography.
3. Arizona—Politics and government. I. Title.
F810 .J64 2002
979.1′05′0922—dc21   2001008029

British Library Cataloguing-in-Publication Data
A catalogue record for this book is available
from the British Library.

To Marilyn and Thayer, who give me strength,
hope, and joy.

Contents

Arizona Politicians

Introduction

Arizona has always been a relatively small state in population, yet it has had an inordinate share of politicians who have gained national attention since statehood in 1912. What caused this phenomenon, and who are these political figures?

Most of them were homegrown, but a few moved to the Grand Canyon state along with thousands of others seeking a new life in the West. Arizona has been described as "a sagebrush hybrid" of veterans, retirees, developers, ranchers, and others who have settled here since World War II. Even today almost 40 percent of the state's five million people lived elsewhere ten years ago. The migration has resulted in a diverse population that caused the state to change from one dominated by Democrats from 1912 to the early 1950s to one run by Republicans in the second half of the twentieth century.

Why has Arizona been blessed with such stalwarts as Barry Goldwater, Stewart and Morris Udall, Sandra Day O'Connor, Bruce Babbitt, Ernest McFarland, John McCain, John Rhodes, and others? An *Arizona Republic* reporter once wondered if it was something in the water, that precious substance politicians fought so long and hard to bring to the arid desert.

The late Congressman Mo Udall saw it this way on a C-Span program with Goldwater in 1985:

> Someone asked me why it was that Arizona, a dinky little state with one percent of the nation's population, produced leaders like John Rhodes and Barry Goldwater, Ernest McFarland and Stew Udall and the others. . . . I said that I seriously didn't know, but that it had something to do with the civilized brand of politics. You go to some states and

your opponent is automatically a thief and a crook and there is little respect for the other side, and I have had a civilized relationship with you, Barry, and John Rhodes and all the people we have mentioned. And I think that's probably the explanation, if there is one.

Udall also said, when Sandra Day O'Connor was nominated to the U.S. Supreme Court, that Arizona had produced more than its share of national politicians because it always "enjoyed a civilized kind of politics. Washington is often confounded at the contrasts, but in Arizona it is taken for granted."

Perhaps it's because Arizona, being one of the last states to join the Union, seems to attract the adventurous, the independent spirit, to its wide-open spaces. Uprooting families and moving to the frontier, which Arizona might seem to be, require risk-taking, and no one ever achieved anything in life without some level of risk.

In its first fifty-five years, Arizona had only seven U.S. senators—Marcus Aurelius Smith, Henry Ashurst, Ralph Cameron, Carl Hayden, Ernest McFarland, Barry Goldwater, and Paul Fannin—and the seniority system being what it was in Congress, those who successfully remained in office came to command great influence.

No state so small has given modern presidential politics such memorable—though never victorious—candidates. They came along every twelve years: Goldwater in 1964, Mo Udall in '76, Babbitt in '88, and McCain in '00. All four candidates used the phrase once coined by Udall's good friend, author Larry L. King, that "Arizona is the only state where mothers don't tell their children they can grow up to be president."

In determining which Arizona politicians should be included in this volume, I looked at a number of factors—national prominence, impact on the state, personality, even notoriety.

Readers might disagree with my choices of whom to include and whom to leave out. In Arizona, as in the rest of the nation, politics has been governed by white males until very recently, and that fact is reflected in the roster of names in this book. Racial and gender discrimination kept many minorities and women on the sidelines from statehood until late in the twentieth century. Some, however, were aggressive enough to break through that discrimination.

Prescott's Sharlot Hall was one. She was appointed territorial historian in 1909. Frances Willard Munds, wife of a Yavapai County rancher and sheriff, was a leader in the women's suffrage movement in Arizona. When she was elected state senator in 1914, she became the second woman in the nation to hold that position. At the same time Rachel Berry of St. Johns became the first woman in the country to serve as a state representative.

Nellie Trent Bush, an airplane and riverboat pilot, was among the first women to attend the University of Arizona Law School. She later served fourteen years in the Arizona house and two in the senate, beginning in 1920. One of her law school classmates was Lorna Lockwood, who later became chief justice of the Arizona Supreme Court, the first woman in the country to serve in such an office. When Elsie Toles was elected state superintendent of public instruction in 1920, she became the first woman to achieve statewide office in Arizona, but she was defeated for reelection two years later.

Polly Rosenbaum, a Democrat from Globe, spent forty-five years in the Arizona House of Representatives before retiring at the age of ninety-five in 1995. Karan English of Flagstaff became only the second woman in Arizona to be elected to the U.S. Congress, serving in the House from 1993 to 1995. Isabella Greenway was the first.

Ana Frohmiller was elected state auditor for twelve straight terms, earning national publicity as the "watchdog of the Arizona treasury." In 1950 she ran for governor on the Democratic ticket, coming within 3,000 votes out of 200,000 cast of being the first woman to hold the post (she lost to Howard Pyle). In his book *Arizona Politics, The Struggle to End One-Party Rule*, Steve Shadegg wrote that when he and a colleague sampled public opinion by visiting Bisbee bars during the campaign, the Democratic bar patrons thought she would lose the race because "Arizona wasn't ready for a woman governor."

That distinction later went to Rose Mofford, although Mofford was not elected to the post. She moved up from secretary of state when Evan Mecham was impeached and removed from office in 1988. Arizona's only other woman governor, Jane Hull, also was not elected initially. She ascended in 1997 when Governor Fife Symington was convicted of bank and wire fraud and resigned from office (his conviction later was overturned and President Clinton pardoned him in 2000). In 1998 she was elected to a full four-year term. As of 1998 only sixteen women in fourteen states had ever served as governor.

In 1975 Margaret Hance was elected mayor of Phoenix, the largest U.S. city to have a woman mayor. The state's second largest city, Tucson, has never had a woman or someone from a racial/ethnic minority group as mayor.

People of color who have served the state are also few, as the chapter on Raul Castro makes clear. The rampant discrimination the former Arizona governor faced throughout his life illustrates why minorities have played such a small role in Arizona's history.

Today the race and gender situation is better, although all of Arizona's seats in Congress are filled by men, and only one, Representative Ed Pastor, is from a minority. One sign of progress is that in 2000 the state's top five elected officials were women: Governor Jane Hull, Attorney General Janet Napolitano, Secretary of State Betsey Bayless, State Superintendent of Public Instruction Lisa Graham Keegan, and Treasurer Carol Springer. (Jaime Molera replaced Keegan in 2001.) In the state's first eighty-eight years, however, only eighteen women have held statewide offices, including the above-named five. Women and minorities are better represented in the state legislature. In 1999 seven of the thirty state senators were women, and twenty-five of the sixty representatives were women.

In Stephen Shadegg's book *Arizona Politics,* published in 1986, more than 180 names are listed in the index, but no more than 10 are women, and some of those are listed because they were married to politicians. You can count on one hand the number of minorities in the index, two of whom are Raul Castro and Cesar Chavez, head of the United Farmer Workers, who was born in Yuma.

The twenty-one politicians profiled in this book were chosen for their contributions to government, for their colorful personalities, and in one or two instances, for their notoriety.

It is interesting that the personal and political lives of so many of these politicians overlap. For example, Goldwater's grandfather put up bail money for Mo and Stewart Udall's grandfather when he was jailed on a trumped-up perjury charge in 1885. Ernest McFarland served on the state supreme court with the Udall brothers' uncle, Jesse Udall, and with Lorna Lockwood in the late 1960s. Raul Castro worked with Mo Udall in the Pima County Attorney's Office in the 1950s. Richard Kleindienst was one of Barry Goldwater's campaign managers. Bruce Babbitt appointed Sandra Day O'Connor to the state appellate court in 1979.

One thing they all have in common, whether natives of the state or transplants, is that they are, or were, proud to call themselves Arizonans, often expressing their love for the state whenever asked. World traveler Lewis Douglas, who was ambassador to Great Britain during the Truman administration, kept his voter registration in the little southern Arizona township of Sonoita. When Mo Udall died, his ashes were scattered in his beloved Catalina Mountains. The state's first governor, George W.P. Hunt, is buried in an odd white pyramid atop a bluff in Phoenix's Papago Park.

Each of the biographies herein is written with some humor, some color, and with a sympathetic view for the subject's accomplishments or foibles. The biographies are arranged in no particular order. I have tried to refresh the reader's memory of renowned figures and then introduced lesser known politicians who might not be as well known today as in their own time. I have also tried to disperse the biographies by race and gender. So the placement of John Rhodes last in the book is not meant to diminish his accomplishments; neither is placing John McCain first meant to elevate him above, say, Barry Goldwater, the Udall brothers, or Sandra Day O'Connor.

John McCain

He has been called the "White Tornado" for the frantic pace he keeps, his hot temper, and the shock of white hair atop his short, injury-scarred body. It's an apt description of Senator John McCain, the fiery former navy pilot and Vietnam prisoner of war. He does everything at almost the supersonic speed of the jet fighters he used to fly.

Passionate, temperamental, and imbued with energy that belies his five and a half years of isolation and torture in North Vietnamese prisons, McCain pursues life on his own terms—

always has, probably always will. With his ability to make enemies as easily as he makes friends, the senator is a love-him-or-hate-him politician who speaks his mind, a characteristic that seems to be shared by Arizonans from the West. But to say that McCain is a true Westerner cast in the mold of Barry Goldwater is to ignore his upbringing.

John Sidney McCain III was born on August 29, 1936, in the Panama Canal Zone, the son and grandson of U.S. Navy admirals. His grandfather graduated 79th in a class of 116 from the Naval Academy and went on to become a pioneer in the development of naval aviation. One of the navy's most respected and decorated admirals, he was aboard the U.S.S. *Missouri* with Admiral Bull Halsey, General Douglas MacArthur, and Admiral Chester Nimitz when the Japanese surrendered to end World War II. His father graduated 423rd out of 441 in the Naval Academy class of 1931 but went on to become commander in chief of U.S. naval forces in Europe and commander in chief of the Pacific. He was the senior military officer in the theater of operations that included North and South Vietnam.

McCain attended private schools while his father was transferred around the world. At the age of twelve, he began to show signs of rebellion. "From that time on, he was a pain the neck," says his mother, Roberta. His classmates called him by such nicknames as Punk, Nasty, or McNasty. "He prided himself on being a tough guy," one classmate told his biographer, Robert Timberg. "He was seemingly ready to fight at the drop of a hat. He was easily provoked, ready to be provoked." When he ran for president in 2000, ABC newscaster Sam Donaldson asked his mother why she was proud of her son. "Because he's such a scamp," she replied.

He wanted to attend Princeton, but it was preordained that he would go to the Naval Academy. "It was part of the air he breathed, the ether through which he moved, the single immutable element in his life," Timberg wrote. According to McCain,

"It was just something that was going to happen. And perhaps that's why I practice this rebellion against the system, always walking the edge." He told *Esquire* magazine, "My life was charted out for me, and I resented that. Not consciously, but clearly subconsciously. You know, ever since I can remember, as a little boy: 'He's going to the Naval Academy.'"

McCain followed in his father's and grandfather's footsteps in more ways than one. He, too, finished in the bottom tier of his class, graduating 894th out of 899 in the class of 1958. It was not that he was such a poor student; his rebellious streak saw him rack up demerit after demerit, but always short of the number to be kicked out. "I hated the place, but I didn't mind going there," he said.

When he graduated, the academy superintendent told his father that McCain was one of his two biggest disappointments at the academy. But the younger McCain, too, was to prove that you do not have to graduate at the top of your class to become successful in the navy. ("I'm the guy that stood fifth from the bottom of his class," he would say years later. "If my old company officer had contemplated that I would make a serious bid for the presidency of the United States, he would have probably had either me or himself committed.") After he graduated, McCain reported for flight training at Pensacola, Florida. During advanced training in Corpus Christi, Texas, his plane's engine quit and the aircraft plunged into the bay. He was knocked unconscious but came to, kicked out the canopy, and fought his way to the surface. He was not injured in this brush with death, one of several during his naval career.

He married Carol Shepp, the divorced mother of two children, Doug and Andy, in July 1965. She gave birth to their daughter, Sidney, in September of 1966, and McCain shipped out on the U.S.S. *Forrestal* in mid-1967.

On July 29, 1967, McCain again escaped serious injury or death while aboard the *Forrestal* as he prepared to take off in his

A-4E Skyhawk, which was sixty miles off the coast of Vietnam. A spark from a generator used to start his engine ignited one of its Zuni rockets, causing a massive explosion. He jumped from the plane, rolled through the fire, and then sprinted away, slapping out flames on his burning uniform. At about that time other rockets began exploding. McCain was struck by shards of metal but was not seriously injured. Others on deck were less fortunate: 134 sailors were killed. The explosion caused $72 million in damage to the *Forrestal,* not counting destroyed aircraft.

Three months later, on October 26, 1967, McCain was part of a twenty-plane mission that set out to hit a power plant in Hanoi. On this mission, his twenty-third, a North Vietnamese missile tore off his right wing, sending his plane down. As Mc-Cain ejected from the cockpit, his knee smashed against the instrument panel. Both arms were broken, apparently by the rushing air, and he parachuted into a small lake in Hanoi. An angry crowd pulled him from the water, and he was spat upon, pummeled, and stabbed with a bayonet in the left ankle and groin. His shoulder was smashed by a rifle butt. Finally, his captors threw him in a truck and hauled him off to prison.

At first McCain was denied medical treatment, but when the North Vietnamese learned he was the son of an admiral, they doctored him up in the most rudimentary of hospitals. To this day he is unable to raise his arms above his shoulders to comb his hair. He spent the next five and a half years as a prisoner of war, including a year of torture and two years of solitary confinement. On one occasion, despite warnings that he would not survive much longer, he refused to be released because other Americans had been held longer.

After his release on March 14, 1973, McCain refused to hold any bitterness. "Nobody made me fly over Vietnam. Nobody drafts you into doing those kinds of things. That's what I was trained to do and that's what I wanted to do."

While in the "Hanoi Hilton," McCain was unaware that his wife Carol had been badly injured when her car skidded out of control on an icy road near her home in Philadelphia. She underwent twenty-three operations and was left severely crippled. The first McCain knew of his wife's condition was on March 14, 1973, when he stepped off a plane in the Philippines.

Like many marriages of prisoners of war, the McCain marriage eventually ended; they separated in 1978 and were divorced in January 1980.

McCain revisited Vietnam in February 2000, the twenty-fifth anniversary of the war's end. "It's always interesting for me to be back here and show my son the place where I lived for a long time," he said in an interview. "But I put Vietnam behind me when I left."

In early 1977 McCain received his first exposure to politics, an experience that would set him off on a new course. He was assigned to be second in command of the navy's Senate liaison office, where he became close friends with Democratic Senator Gary Hart of Colorado and Republican Senator William Cohen of Maine. Not long after, on a trip to Hawaii, he met Cindy Hensley, the daughter of a wealthy Phoenix beer distributor, who was seventeen years his junior. They were married in May 1980 and have four children: Meghan, Jack, Jim, and Bridget.

In March 1981, about the time his father died, McCain retired from the navy as a captain. He had been awarded the Silver Star, Bronze Star, Legion of Merit, Purple Heart, and Distinguished Flying Cross. Now he was ready to embark on a new career—politics. He moved to Phoenix, took a public relations job with his father-in-law's distributorship, and began staking out his political future. He wanted to run for Congress, and the chance came in January 1982, when fellow Republican and House Minority Leader John Rhodes, who had held the seat for three decades, decided to retire.

McCain pounded the pavement, knocking on 20,000 doors during a primary campaign in which he was pitted against three popular candidates. He had to answer charges that he was a carpetbagger, but he told all who would listen that the place he had lived longest in his life was Hanoi. He won the primary in the heavily Republican district by getting 32 percent of the vote, with the next closest candidate receiving 26 percent. The general election was no contest, and he won by a margin of 35 percentage points.

In 1984 McCain won reelection, then decided to seek the Senate seat held by the retiring Barry Goldwater in 1986. When Goldwater told him, "If I'd won [the presidency], you never would've spent all those years in a North Vietnamese prison camp," McCain replied, "You're right, Barry. It would've been a Chinese prison camp."

Democratic Governor Bruce Babbitt also had his eye on the seat, thinking it could be a stepping stone in his run for the presidency in 1988. Ultimately, Babbitt decided against entering the race, perhaps believing he could not beat the popular McCain in a highly Republican state, and thereby hurt his chances of winning the Democratic presidential nomination in 1988.

With Babbitt out of the way, McCain received token opposition from an Arizona Corporation Commission member, Richard Kimball, a Robert Redford look-alike, whom he beat by a 57 to 43 percent margin. As he took office, speculation was rampant that McCain might be a possible running mate for George Bush during the 1988 election, but Bush chose Indiana Senator Dan Quayle.

As fast as McCain's star had risen, it started to slip in October 1989. He ran into trouble because of his relationship with Charles Keating, the embattled savings-and-loan kingpin, who had contributed $112,000 to his House and Senate campaigns. McCain would call it "the worst thing, the absolute worst thing that ever happened to me," a claim that is astonishing in light of his Vietnam experience.

He was one of a group that the media dubbed "the Keating Five," who had allegedly put pressure on officials of the Federal Home Loan Bank Board to help Keating, who was under investigation in the failure of his Lincoln Savings and Loan Association. After almost eighteen agonizing months, however, the Senate Ethics Committee handed down the most mild of rebukes to McCain, accusing him of poor judgment, a vindication of serious wrongdoing. The scandal did little to hurt him, and he won reelection in 1992 by a whopping 58 percent of the vote in a three-way race.

During his second term, McCain took on two major issues— reform of campaign finance laws and anti-tobacco legislation— issues he is still fighting for today. Thanks to his temper during these fights, he earned the nickname of "Senator Hothead." In 1996 speculation arose about McCain becoming running mate for Republican nominee Bob Dole. Again he was passed over, this time for former Congressman Jack Kemp.

In 1997 McCain began taking steps to improve his own presidential hopes in 2000, but first he had to win reelection, which he did with 70 percent of the vote. That included 65 percent of the women's vote, 55 percent of the Hispanic vote, and 40 percent of the Democratic vote.

He knew if he were to run for president, he would have to address such personal issues as whether he was physically and mentally healthy. In December 1999 he released 1,500 pages of medical and psychiatric records in which doctors said he was in good health on both counts. The file was extensive because it was standard procedure for POWs to undergo psychological evaluations after their release. One report said he had "adjusted exceptionally well to repatriation" and had "an ambitious, striving, successful pattern of adjustment."

Soon after his release from captivity, Dr. P. F. O'Connell, a navy physician, wrote that from the time McCain realized he was the son of a famous, highly successful naval officer, although proud of his father, he had been preoccupied with escaping from the shadow of his own image, the way that others viewed him. "He feels his experiences and performance as a P.O.W. have finally permitted this to happen. It was with a smile of fulfillment and relief and a wink at his father that he enjoyed hearing [him] being introduced at a public dinner as 'Commander McCain's father.' He had arrived."

During the campaign for his party's nomination, McCain was forced to deal with criticism of his anger. On ABC's *Good Morning America,* he said: "I'm very comfortable that I feel strongly about issues of right and wrong and have a passion about it. I have gotten angry at people. And I will probably continue to get angry when I see an injustice done. I feel that, as I say, people who aren't represented and people who are not well treated, particularly in the legislative process, deserve that kind of attention. And I'll continue to give it."

On another occasion he remarked in campaign rhetoric: "People say that perhaps John McCain gets angry. My friends, I get angry when we spend $350 million on a carrier the Navy doesn't want or need, $500-and-some million on an airplane, a C-130, that the Air Force has said for years they don't need. And meanwhile, my dear friends, we have 12,000 enlisted families on food stamps. That's a disgrace."

Another time he admitted: "There are things that make me mad. I do everything I can to keep my anger under control. I wake up daily and tell myself, 'You must do everything possible to stay cool, calm, and collected today.' "

McCain became the media darling during the presidential campaign. He had learned a lesson from his friend Mo Udall about getting the media on his side. He traveled in a campaign bus called the Straight Talk Express and invited reporters to ride with him. They liked his position on campaign reform and his fight against the tobacco industry. Steve Wilson, a columnist for the *Arizona Republic,* said, "His impish personality and moderate political views play well across party lines." He called McCain "unscripted, entertaining, the underdog, experienced, a war hero and electable."

He knew he was up against a formidable candidate in George W. Bush, the Texas governor and son of the former president. Although he pulled off a major upset by beating Bush in New Hampshire by 19 percentage points, McCain could not sustain the momentum. He did manage to win seven primaries, including his home state's, but the result was only 160 delegate votes out of a possible 2,066. Bush won the nomination, and talk turned to the vice presidency.

McCain had appealed to independent voters, and Bush needed to make inroads with them. He decided, however, to go with party loyalty in picking his father's former defense secretary, Dick Cheney. He knew McCain could not be trusted to toe the party line.

McCain has hinted that this might be his last term in office. "I can see myself believing that eighteen years in the Senate is enough. If you can't accomplish what you want to accomplish in eighteen years, then you probably are not going to in six more years after that." Even so, he still clings to presidential hopes. His chances to achieve the White House were set back when Bush won the presidency. But should Bush falter—Bush and McCain were never close—McCain could be ready to step into a race in 2004, the last year of his Senate term.

Isabella Greenway

Isabella Greenway brought attention to Arizona in three ways: she was the first woman to serve in Congress from the Grand Canyon state (and only one of two overall), she was a close friend of Eleanor Roosevelt, and she founded the widely acclaimed Arizona Inn in Tucson.

Greenway was the lone lawmaker from Arizona in the House of Representatives from 1933 to 1937, a period when few women had ever served in the Congress. Three other women were in the House with Greenway, and only sixteen other women had served before her. She owed her seat to Arizona's heavily Democratic voter registration and to her alignment with the Roosevelt administration during the New Deal years.

She was born on March 22, 1880, in Boone County, Kentucky, to Tilden and Martha Selmes. Her father was a Yale-educated lawyer who once worked for an old friend, Abraham Lincoln, in his law office. Selmes later established a sheep and horse ranch in South Dakota but left to return to law in St. Paul, Minnesota. When her father died, fifteen-year-old Isabella and her mother moved to New York City, where she entered a finishing school for young women.

One of her classmates was Eleanor Roosevelt, and Isabella eventually would be a bridesmaid when Eleanor married the future president. At the age of nineteen, Isabella married Robert Ferguson, a Rough Rider and close friend of the Roosevelts, who was fifteen years her senior. They honeymooned in Scotland, where they were joined by Eleanor and Franklin, who had been married the previous March. Isabella became godmother of the Roosevelts' first child, Anna, and she and Robert had two children, Martha and Robert Jr. After ten years of marriage, Ferguson contracted tuberculosis. In hopes of improving his health, the family moved to Silver City, New Mexico, where he lived thirteen more years before his death in 1922.

During World War I Isabella served as chairwoman of the Women's Land Army of New Mexico, an organization that placed women in jobs ordinarily held by men. After her husband's death, she moved to Santa Barbara, California, and within a year married Colonel John C. Greenway, another Rough Rider and a close friend of Ferguson, and they moved to Ajo, Arizona, to operate a copper mine.

Three years later, after the birth of a third child, John, Isabella Greenway found herself a widow again when her husband died while undergoing surgery. Ferguson had left her with a modest estate, and when he died Greenway left a substantial estate, so she was financially secure. Shortly after her husband's death, she founded the Arizona Hut, a craft shop run by disabled veterans who produced bead and leather work, and furniture. She financed the operation with copper stock she and her husband had accumulated, but the enterprise lost $30,000 in its first two years. She never made money on the Hut and closed it in September 1933.

Just before the Great Depression, Greenway sold her copper stock against the advice of friends and built the stately Arizona Inn, one of Tucson's oldest and grandest resorts; it still attracts visitors from around the world, including the powerful and the wealthy. A friend told the *Arizona Daily Star,* "Her aim was to have it as homelike as possible, and to permit privacy so guests would have as much chance to live in a hotel as they would in their home. She very much liked putting up guests, especially her friends, many of whom were celebrities, and they never were exploited." The inn, which is listed in the National Register of Historic Places, has been called one of the ten best country inns in America.

Greenway's early interest in politics resurfaced, and she was elected as a Democratic national committeewoman from Arizona. In 1928 she campaigned for Democratic nominee Alfred E. Smith against eventual winner Herbert Hoover and found herself being mentioned as a potential gubernatorial candidate. Franklin Roosevelt wrote her in 1929: "I have a rather definite suggestion that you should seriously consider the possibility of allowing the use of your name for the Governorship of Arizona next fall. Apparently people are getting rather tired of the factional disturbances caused by the perennial candidacy of Governor [George W.P.] Hunt and feel that you would satisfy all factions. More than that, they say that you would make a splendid Governor—and that, after all, is the most important of all." She decided against the suggestion and worked within the party to help Roosevelt in his 1932 presidential bid.

At the Democratic convention in Chicago, she seconded the motion to make her old friend the nominee. She was asked to give the five-minute seconding speech because of her hard work for Roosevelt in Arizona and because of their long relationship. Also because of her work, the Arizona delegation nominated her for vice president during the convention, but Greenway made it clear that the gesture was simply honorary.

The *New York Times* called her "the most-talked of woman at the National Democratic Convention." She was mentioned as a possible candidate for a job in the new Roosevelt administration, but then Arizona Congressman Lewis W. Douglas resigned to become the new administration's budget director. It was likely a Democrat would win his seat in the special election because the state and national offices were dominated by Democrats, so Greenway decided to run. And her strong ties to the Roosevelts surely were helpful.

Greenway faced two well-known Democrats who had run in the 1932 election—Phoenix attorney Harlow Akers, who earlier had challenged Senator Carl Hayden, and William Coxon, former secretary of the Arizona Corporation Commission, who had run against Douglas. Governor Hunt remained neutral in the race but noted privately, "Mrs. Greenway will probably get elected with her money, but we do not need a society woman in Congress."

Greenway campaigned throughout the state in her tri-motored airplane, using her finishing school charm to win over voters. The press praised her sincerity, ability, intelligence, unselfish public record, party loyalty, and personality. She refused to get drawn into a debate over her wealth, viewing it as an advantage that gave her "a peculiar strength in being able to keep an honest faith in the field of politics."

Greenway won 70 percent of the primary vote and faced token opposition in the general election. To oppose her the Socialist Party nominated Dillworth Sumpter and the Republican State Central Committee drafted H. B. Wilkinson, Douglas's old Republican opponent. Greenway pulled 73 percent of the vote and the Socialist finished second, an indication of how poorly Republicans rated in Arizona. Arizonans, no doubt, were impressed by her close friendship with the new occupants of the White House.

Her intention was to give her support to Roosevelt, but not long after she went to Washington, she realized that she would be at odds with some of the president's programs. She often called meetings of other members of Congress from the West to attempt to override Roosevelt's vetoes.

Greenway's independence received great attention from the press. A 1935 *New York Times* article noted:

> From the moment early in the present session when Mrs. Greenway seemed to plant her feet composedly on the marble floors of the Capitol, she has pursued a definitely, if not unostentatiously, independent course of action in matters of program and facts, which leaves the mere political experts increasingly mystified. . . . Powerful House committees have heard Mrs. Greenway's pleas for solutions of the problems of the small-home owner, the underprivileged and the distressed on more comprehensive and often more expensive terms than the White House and its Congressional advisors have been willing to sanction. Privately, several of the leaders of the "big committees" have had the experience of not being quite able to dispose of a charming, determined and strangely convincing woman who insists on believing, in defiance of "practical" politics, that the New Deal in its social advances must continue to tax and spend with gallantry. The White House, too, almost certainly heard these same arguments in the quiet atmosphere of friendship.

Perhaps she got that independence from her experiences in the West. She told the *New York Times,* "People don't look at those gaunt mountains and those sunsets out there without becoming different persons. People don't hitch their horses under a cottonwood tree and stay on . . . to build a ranch or perhaps even a city . . . without getting a new set of values. . . . The West is so much less afraid of the things we may have to do and the changes we may have to make in order to save the values in American life that are worth saving that sometimes I think this courage of the West to dare new adventures . . . may be our final salvation."

She also felt she had to explain to Franklin Roosevelt why she was breaking with him. In an April 30, 1934, letter, she wrote:

> It is inevitable that you and Eleanor will frequently be embarrassed with doubts about my loyalty, and convictions as to my bad judgment. This I have accepted and I am going to try to stop worrying over the distasteful intrigue and political pressure that would well undermine our cherished family relations. The long pull will tell the tale and while I have too few opportunities to discuss these things with you and do not believe your time should be asked—I am going to weather hurt, mistrust and criticism, and assume that eight years from now we will come out on the other side of this ghastly experience—happy and united.

Greenway knew well the value of honesty with her constituents. In a letter to a friend, she wrote, "One of the greatest mistakes I believe our leaders have fallen into over a long period of years is in failing to tell the people how serious their difficulties are, how hard it may be to remedy them. I think I know something about the people. I believe they are not only anxious to know the truth and will welcome it but that they have the courage to face it, whatever it is."

She decided against seeking a third term, announcing that

she was fatigued and that she needed to attend to her business of operating the Arizona Inn. In making the announcement, she said, "The advent of the fiftieth year is surprisingly thrilling. I'll tell you how it feels. You come face to face with the fact that you're crazy to live. You begin to budget your resources with an eagerness akin to greed, and all the while you discover how generous beyond any desserts, are the compensations of our good providence."

When she left office, some felt that differences between her and the Roosevelt administration were the major reason, according to her biographer Betty Morrison. Morrison said Greenway was frustrated by her inability to circumvent petty bureaucrats, and she desired a fuller personal life.

It wasn't until 1992 that another woman from Arizona, Karan English, would be elected to Congress. English served one term before she was defeated in her bid to return to the House. No woman has been elected since.

When Roosevelt sought a third term, Greenway stunned her party by supporting the Republican nominee, Wendell L. Willkie. She opposed a third term for any president. She was quoted as saying:

> All the powers needed to create a dictator have been granted now. Should I be specific? . . . Our President has appointed the majority of the Supreme Court, five out of nine; he is head of the army and navy; one-fourth of the inhabitants of this country receive entire or partial government benefits, directly or indirectly, from his subordinates; he has more positions to fill, more money to give and lend, more authority to enact and enforce regulatory laws and has the sum total of powers granted to him by Congress over the last eight years, none of which has ever been recalled, which give him, or his successor, the absolute power of a dictator.

After leaving Congress, Greenway became the national chairwoman of the American Women's Volunteer Services and a trustee of the Tucson Desert Sanitarium, later to become Tucson Medical Center. In 1939 she married Harry King and continued to operate the Arizona Inn.

She died of a heart attack on December 18, 1953, at the age of seventy-three.

Stewart Udall

In the mid-1950s, Stewart Udall became acquainted with a handsome young senator from Massachusetts who had presidential ambitions. When the senator, John Kennedy, sought the Democratic nomination for the presidency in 1960, Udall helped deliver Arizona's delegates. After he was elected, the grateful Kennedy named Udall to be secretary of interior, the first Arizonan to hold a cabinet position.

It was a long way from the serene farm life in the Mormon community of St. Johns, Arizona, where Stewart Lee Udall was born on January 31, 1920, to the inner circles of the White House. When Kennedy was assassinated, it was generally assumed that President Lyndon Johnson would appoint a new interior secretary. But Udall had conceived the idea of beautifying the nation's capital by planting hundreds of flower beds and had sold the idea to Lady Bird Johnson. She got the credit, and Udall kept his job. He was one of only four cabinet members left over from the Kennedy administration.

"As a politician, I was able to catch the right wind," he remarked.

Udall undertook stewardship of the land in part because of his upbringing in St. Johns. "I grew up in barren country—juniper, piñon, high plateau," he said in a 1973 interview, "—so even with a little dam and irrigation, we learned the importance of water. There's a tie to the land. And there wasn't a long growing season. When you had a late [cold] front, you lost your fruit crop. That was something you lived with. When people ask me how I became a conservationist, I tell them I grew up that way."

"The Mormon village is a place where religion is very strong and forms the matrix of life. When you spend your formative years [there] . . . you know and learn a lot about human nature and human beings and values," he told the author in 1998.

Describing his early experiences, he wrote in 1982:

The Mormons knew the importance of water, and wherever they settled they built dams and canals to make irrigated farming possible. Every boy in St. Johns learned to work with water at an early age. I can still hear my father telling me earnestly, "Irrigation is a science, son. . . ."

Modernization rode a slow horse to St. Johns. . . .

I am forced to concede that our outdoor toilets were crude and inconvenient. However, even this famous piece of nineteenth-century architecture had one great advantage over the flush toilets and defective sewage disposal system which superseded it. We buried our wastes in the earth. They did not contaminate our rivers. As the Little Colorado passed St. Johns, it had swimming holes that were clean and fish-life that was edible. . . .

Our lives made us natural conservationists.

Udall's father, Levi, was an Apache County Superior Court judge who later became chief justice of the Arizona Supreme Court. His brother Morris served thirty years in Congress and unsuccessfully sought the 1976 Democratic nomination for president.

"I stood on my father's shoulders. Morris stood on his shoulders," Udall would say later. He described his father as a "rippling circle outward. . . . Public service was kind of a religion with Dad. . . . I was taught that a person may aspire to nothing higher than to be a public servant. . . . Some of my liberalism and feelings about being champion of the underdog came from mother."

As a youngster, Udall learned how to dress a hog, mend a roof, and practice the craft of stone masonry. He played on school basketball, football, and tennis teams and served as freshman class president in St. Johns. After graduation he attended Eastern Arizona Junior College in Thatcher for a year in 1937, then transferred to the University of Arizona. He took a break from school to serve his two-year Mormon mission in New York and Pennsylvania, the only one of three Udall boys to do so. Then it was off to war, where he served in the air corps as a B-24 gunner, completing fifty missions over Europe and earning the Air Medal with three oak leaf clusters.

After the war Udall returned to the University of Arizona to study law. In an early effort in his lifelong crusade to end racial discrimination, he and brother Morris helped integrate a university dining facility. They also "began agitation" about the absence of blacks on athletic teams at the university, a situation that was finally remedied in the 1951–52 school year. A proficient basketball player himself, Udall was a guard on the first UA team to play in the National Invitational Tournament in Madison Square Garden.

After earning his law degree in 1948, he established a practice in Tucson and helped found the Tucson Council for Civic Unity, a group that worked to end segregation in the city. Lunch counters in Tucson were segregated, and he helped talk the owner of five or six drugstores into allowing blacks to eat there. The owner said he would but asked the Udalls not to "make a fuss about it."

He married Erma Lee Webb in 1947, and they had six children: Tom, Scott, Lynn, Lori, Denis, and James. One of them, Tom, now represents a New Mexico district in the U.S. House of Representatives.

Brother Mo became partners with Stewart in the law firm in 1949. "We flipped a coin for opening and closing statements," Stewart said. But, in fact, Stewart was better at pretrial homework and Morris at courtroom theatrics.

During the late 1940s and early '50s, Stewart Udall became active in politics, serving as vice chairman of the Democratic Party's central committee, treasurer of the Pima County Legal Aid Society, and president of the Amphitheater school board. When Harold A. "Porque" Patten decided against seeking another term in the U.S. House of Representatives, Udall jumped into the race in 1954 and defeated Henry Zipf, 68,085 to 41,587. He got off to a fast start when he was the only freshman selected by House Speaker Sam Rayburn to serve on the six-member House delegation at the first NATO parliamentary conference in 1955.

Voters at home seemed pleased with Udall's work, electing him three more times before he was appointed to the cabinet.

He was instrumental in securing passage of the legislation that created the Glen Canyon Dam and situating the town of Page on the Arizona side of the dam. (Later he regretted damming the

Colorado River. "Glen Canyon Dam was a mistake. It should have been a national park," he said.) In 1958 he sponsored a bill authorizing the Papago (now Tohono O'odham) tribe to lease 2,400 acres at Kitt Peak to the National Science Foundation.

Along with George McGovern of South Dakota and Gene McCarthy of Minnesota, Udall helped found the Democratic Study Group, which worked toward the reform of Congress, particularly attacking the seniority system. "There's a tradition in the House that new members should not be heard. But if you are not heard in the first two years, you may never be heard at all," he said.

As the thirty-seventh interior secretary at the age of forty-one, he was in charge of 65,000 employees and an $800 million budget. Interior's responsibilities included nearly 600 million acres of federal land, more than a fourth of the land in the United States.

In accepting the appointment, Udall said he had cast his lot with Kennedy "for the reason that I saw in him the personal character and talents of leadership I thought our country needed at this time." He said he was happy to serve as interior secretary because "few areas in government leave a more abiding and visible mark on our land and our individual future than what is done or not done by the Department of Interior. . . . Kennedy didn't know anybody in the West much, but he liked me. I earned the appointment because I helped him at a crucial time."

During his eight-year cabinet career, Udall pushed legislation setting aside 9.2 million acres of wilderness land, mostly in the West, and establishing the Wild and Scenic Rivers Act. He oversaw the expansion of the National Park System to include four new national parks, six national monuments, eight sea and lake shores, nine recreation areas, twenty historic sites, and fifty-six wildlife refuges, and the creation of the Land and Water Conservation Fund.

In 1963 he published his first book, *The Quiet Crisis*, which became a bestseller. In it he traced American environmental attitudes and practices and pointed to the wisdom of Native Americans, who "understood that we are not outside nature, but of it." He wrote the book by getting up at three or four o'clock in the morning and writing in longhand at home before going to the office.

Udall even used his power to advance integration. In 1962 he told George P. Marshall, owner of the Washington Redskins football team, that the Redskins were welcome to play in the newly built stadium in Washington, D.C., if they became an integrated team. The stadium had been built with federal funds and was situated on land under the jurisdiction of the Department of the Interior. Marshall agreed.

Udall has been rated as one of the better men to have held the post of interior secretary. John Saylor, the ranking Republican in the House Interior Committee, said in 1969, "It has been the greatest eight years since Teddy Roosevelt. There has been more positive action taken to set aside areas for people than ever before. Mr. Udall, as far as leadership was concerned, was way ahead of Congress."

Quick to admit mistakes, including approval of the Santa Barbara Channel oil leases, Udall also noted, "We broke a lot of new ground in terms of conservation and land use policy, but the other thing which may be more important historically was in our orchestrating the beginning of the modern environmental movement."

In 1968 Udall was instrumental in securing passage of legislation establishing the Central Arizona Project to bring Colorado River water to the arid desert for agricultural use. He later regretted support of the CAP but also pointed out that for all Arizona legislators the "political hair was short" on the issue. "No water, and you're dead politically," he said. He began to have doubts while serving years later on the CAP board, contending the project had been built to provide water to farmers, not to municipalities.

On some issues his views changed 180 degrees during his eight-year tenure as interior secretary. "I began with the idea that dams were probably a good thing," he explained. "I presumed that if anyone, the Corps of Engineers, the Bureau of Reclamation, wanted to build a dam, it was a good thing. I ended up thinking that we ought to be highly skeptical of any dams. I began feeling that we ought to build more roads in national parks, and I ended up believing that we ought to stop building them."

After leaving office, Udall remained in Washington, where he wrote books, articles, and newspaper columns and gave speeches and lectures on issues connected with the environment and natural resources. In his book *1976: Agenda for Tomorrow,* he argued that cities should be considered as environment and suggested that cleaning urban areas become a national project: "The worst environments of this country are the slums of the big cities and work places—everything from the coal mines to the chemical plants, where people live part of their lives or all of their lives. Our environmental priorities ought to begin with the slums of the cities and move out to the wilderness and not vice versa."

In 1968 he thought about running for the Senate seat vacated by the retiring Carl Hayden, but Barry Goldwater was seeking a return to the Senate after sitting out four years following his failed bid for the presidency. Udall doubted he could beat Goldwater. So he continued his life of practicing law and writing and speaking on the environment. In 1974 he wrote *The Energy Balloon,* a detailed analysis of the nation's wasteful energy habits and the steps needed to correct them.

From 1970 to 1972 he wrote a national syndicated column, *Udall on the Environment.* In 1971 he published *America's Natural Treasures: National Nature Monuments and Seashores* and became an adviser to McGovern during his presidential campaign in 1972. Then he managed brother Morris Udall's unsuccessful campaign for the Democratic presidential nomination in 1976.

In 1978 he became the lead lawyer against the federal government on behalf of a group of Navajo Indians who mined uranium but had not been warned of the dangers they faced from exposure to the radioactive ore. He also represented a group of "downwinders," people who lived in Nevada, Utah, and the Arizona Strip during atmospheric atomic bomb testing in Nevada. Eventually he also represented workers from the Nevada Test Site. He fought the battle for twelve years. His son Tom and daughter Lori, who later served with the Environmental Defense Fund in Washington, D.C., cut their legal teeth helping him with the case. He lost when the Supreme Court ruled the government was protected by sovereign immunity.

Unwilling to accept the Court's decision, he took the issue to Congress, and in 1990 President Bush signed into law a bill that compensated the downwinders. Udall had taken the cases on a contingency fee basis, paid for the expenses through fundraising and out of his own pocket, and for years received no legal fees. He now is being paid out of the compensation program that came from the legislation.

Udall supported Rep. John Anderson's unsuccessful bid for the presidency on the Independent ticket in 1980. In 1986 he decided against running for Congress in Arizona's Fourth District, for the seat vacated by Eldon Rudd. "I saw myself as a one-term truth-teller who could make each member of Congress feel responsible for his or her part of the national debt. My fantasies were short-lived. A visit to Washington convinced me it was foolish to think that one angry old-timer could make a difference."

In 1986, he won the Ansel Adams Award, the Wilderness Society's highest conservation award. King Juan Carlos of Spain knighted him in 1989 for his book *To the Inland Empire.* "It's an interesting business. I'm kind of a bleacher Mormon and here they make me a Spanish knight. But I admire King Juan Carlos. He's the most important king in about 350 years for Spain. So I said I would be very flattered to accept the honor," he said at the time.

Udall now lives in Santa Fe, New Mexico, where he is still an active speaker and writer. When Barry Goldwater wrote him a letter in 1989 about hating to see him leave Arizona, he replied: "Barry, I haven't really gone. I guess I'm kind of like an Indian—a citizen of the region."

On another occasion he remarked, "The state lines the white man drew didn't really ever make much difference to me. My ties are to the land and the culture, rather than any state per se. Phoenix just got to be too much. It's becoming another Los Angeles. Here, we [he and his wife, Lee] love to sit on our hill and watch the sunsets and feed the birds."

Evan Mecham

Evan Mecham may have brought more notoriety or discredit to Arizona than any other politicians, most of whom have been either oddballs, dedicated public servants, or lackluster seat warmers. Yet he continues to have his passel of supporters who believe a grand conspiracy drove him from the office of governor.

He was the subject of ridicule, scorn, and even anger during the two years leading to his impeachment and removal from office in the late 1980s. His actions caused former U.S. Senator Barry Goldwater to remark, "We've had some damn good [governors], we've had some mediocre ones, but it took us a long time to get a really bad one."

Mecham's insensitivity toward minorities, his high-handed political activities, and his inability to recognize his shortcomings often made him a laughingstock. He gave new meaning to the term "gadfly," thanks to his mostly unsuccessful forays for political office. His appearance and personality made him the butt of numerous jokes. A slight man at five-foot-six and 138 pounds, he wore an ill-fitting hairpiece. Sam Steiger, who was special assistant to Mecham, said most of the criticism of the governor had to do with his style, "like his toupee, his inappropriate grammar . . . the idea that he's overly simplistic . . . his unwillingness to compromise."

Nonetheless, he had a loyal following among the extreme right wing of the Republican Party, senior citizens, and members of the Church of Jesus Christ of Latter-day Saints, of which he was a member. Mormons make up about 15 percent of the population of Arizona, senior citizens 11 percent, and right-wingers about 5 percent.

Evan "Ev" Mecham (pronounced MEE-kum) was born May 12, 1924, in Duchenne County, in the northeast corner of Utah, where his ancestors had homesteaded 160 acres. His parents were not poor, but neither were they prosperous. They raised alfalfa, wheat, barley, and corn, as well as twenty-five purebred Holstein cows. Evan graduated from Altamont High School, where he did well in the Future Farmers of America and won a Sears Roebuck scholarship that allowed him to enroll at Utah State Agricultural College, now Utah State University. He attended for only a few months before enlisting in the army air corps in January 1943 during World War II.

Mecham trained to become a pilot at bases in Arizona and was decorated with the Air Medal and Purple Heart for action in Europe. When the war was over, he returned home, where he married his high school sweetheart, Florence Lambert, in

1945 and sold insurance. The couple would have seven children: Suzanne, Dennis, Christine, Eric, Teresa, Kyle, and Lance.

In 1947 they moved to Arizona, as did many servicemen who had spent time in the Grand Canyon state during the war. Mecham attended Arizona State College, now Arizona State University, from 1947 to 1950, majoring in management and economics. He dropped out sixteen units short of graduation to open Mecham Pontiac and Rambler in Ajo, Arizona. His advertising motto was "If you can't deal with Mecham, you just can't deal." In 1952 he made his first bid for public office, losing a race in Ajo for the state house of representatives. In 1954 he relocated to Glendale.

As Ronald J. Watkins, author of *High Crimes and Misdemeanors,* wrote, Mecham appeared regularly on television in thirty-second spots, eighty-three words, hawking his cars. "He had a pleasant and easy manner. He looked directly into the lens, and the viewer felt as if Ev Mecham were speaking to him. He was soothing and calm, a polished huckster."

The initial car business grew into other family-owned businesses, including Mecham Racing, Hauahaupan Mining Company, and several dealerships in other states. Mecham was president and chairman of the board of Mecham Pontiac until the dealership was sold in 1988.

The television appearances gave him recognition that helped him win election to a two-year term in the state senate in 1960. Two years later he ran against Carl Hayden for the U.S. Senate and lost badly. He received little or no help from Republican leaders, who recognized the value of Hayden's thirty-five years of Senate seniority if the proposed Central Arizona Project, the multibillion-dollar water plan, were ever to be constructed. He said he received less than $20,000 from the party and that Goldwater had promised to raise $50,000 for him. "His endorsement of my candidacy amounted to a lot of damnation with a bit of faint praise," Mecham said. The *Arizona Republic* editorialized that

Hayden had to be reelected so that the CAP could be approved. That, Mecham said, was why he lost.

Angry at the establishment media, he began publishing his own tabloid newspaper, *The Evening American,* "A Straight-Shooting Newspaper," in 1963. For the next decade it was known for its conservative views and challenges to business and political leaders, a theme Mecham's political campaigns embodied.

Undiscouraged by his first political defeat, Mecham decided to run for governor in 1964, one of six times he would bid to be the state's chief executive. He ran for public office so many times he was often called the Harold Stassen of Arizona. In the Republican primary he ran against the "establishment" by taking on Richard Kleindienst, a longtime associate of Goldwater. Kleindienst won the primary but lost the general election to Sam Goddard. He blamed the loss on Mecham because of the bitter primary battle.

Mecham dropped out of politics for the next decade, but in 1974 he got the bug again, becoming one of five candidates in the Republican primary for governor. Russ Williams, a member of the Arizona Corporation Commission, won the primary but then lost to Democrat Raul Castro, the first Hispanic to hold the governor's chair. As he was wont to do, Mecham blamed his loss on the press for giving him unfair coverage.

Castro quit after two years to become ambassador to El Salvador and was succeeded by Secretary of State Wesley Bolin, but Bolin died before his term was over. Next in the line of succession was Attorney General Bruce Babbitt, who served out the term and then sought election to the post in 1978.

Mecham decided again to run for governor. He won the Republican primary, but even though he lost the general election to the Notre Dame/Harvard–educated Babbitt, the margin was far closer than predicted. Mecham garnered 46 percent of the vote. The closeness of the race prompted one prominent Arizona

Republican to remark, "There are a lot more bowling alleys in Arizona than sushi bars." Mecham blamed his loss on his inability to get his message out because he lacked funds.

In 1982 he ran again. During that campaign he wrote a campaign autobiography, *Come Back America,* in which he said the country had been "led to the edge of . . . moral and economic bankruptcy" by fifty years of socialism manipulated by unidentified "Master Planners." He wrote, "It appeared that the Master Planners decided [during the environmental crisis] the other sure way to bring America to her knees was to make us dependent on foreign sources of energy. To help this along, nuclear energy, originally developed in the U.S., made much more progress abroad because of government, ecologists, and soft-headed judges."

Similar problems had beset the auto industry, he argued. "Some feel that there was a great conspiracy to kill off the U.S. car industry in order to kill the U.S. economy. Out of the resulting economic chaos the Socialists would finish destroying the Republic and emerge with a Socialist Dictatorship in complete control. . . . Whether it was the case, events have fit the scenario."

America had a religious and moral superiority, he said, that gave it a "manifest destiny to lead mankind out of the darkness of ignorance, tyranny, slavery and starvation into the glorious light of freedom, abundance, continual progress. . . . Almost everything about our history bears out the guiding hand of a loving God."

Mecham was beaten in the primary by Senate President Leo Corbet. His defeat was so thorough he announced he would never again run for public office. "I gave the Evan Mecham version of Nixon's 'You're not gonna have me to kick around any more' press conference and thoroughly enjoyed it," he said.

But there was still some fight left in the perennial candidate. When Babbitt announced he would not seek reelection so he could run for the presidency, Mecham jumped into the race. He said he had not meant it when he had said he was quitting politics. His candidacy was greeted as that of an all-time loser and generally disregarded.

To win the Republican primary, he had to beat Senate Majority Leader Burton Barr, one of the most influential legislators in the previous twenty years. At midyear Barr was favored by 40 percent of the voters and Mecham by 5 percent. The rest were undecided. Said Steiger, who would become a Mecham aide, "It's not socially acceptable in some circles to admit you're voting for Evan Mecham."

Barr outspent Mecham four to one and had a fifteen-point lead in the polls on primary election day. "Absolutely nobody expected him to win," said John Kolbe, political columnist for the *Phoenix Gazette.* "It just couldn't happen. We all knew it couldn't happen." But it did. He won with 54 percent of the vote. "Burton Barr," Mecham said, "represented everything I despised about Arizona politics. He'd wielded his authority in the state legislature to enrich himself and his friends, while giving lip service to the needs of the state."

Then Mecham won the 1986 general election with 40 percent of the vote in a three-way race with Democrat Carolyn Warner, former state superintendent of public instruction, and third-party candidate Bill Schulz, a multimillionaire developer. Some said Schulz drew votes away from Warner, thereby giving the election to Mecham. But Warner's pollster found that even without Schulz, the race would have been a "dead heat."

Arizona history would never be the same with Mecham in the governor's office. After being sworn in, he said, "We have to completely reorganize the government because it has been essentially not operated for the last decade." When he submitted his first budget, it was only 67 pages long, compared to the detailed 300-plus-page document the previous year. It stripped lawmakers of much of their power to dictate how state funds were spent and put it in the hands of department heads, many of them controlled by the governor.

"He was, and remains, convinced that the state is controlled by an exclusive coterie of power brokers whose handsome bank-rolls manipulate lawmakers to increase their own wealth at the expense of the average working man and woman," wrote Dave Nichols, who was a TV newscaster when Mecham was governor. "Mecham understands that there is a huge reservoir of people who feel anger toward the system, who think government does things to them, not for them," said House Minority Leader Art Hamilton, a Democrat, in 1987.

Mecham fulfilled his campaign promise to cancel the state holiday honoring Dr. Martin Luther King, Jr., which prompted eight organizations to cancel Arizona conventions in protest and the National Football League to cancel the 1993 Super Bowl in Arizona.

Mecham said he eliminated the holiday because he had been told by Republican Attorney General Bob Corbin that it was illegal. Babbitt had proclaimed the holiday on the third Monday of January after the legislature turned it down. Corbin told Mecham and Barr that whoever was elected would have to rescind the proclamation because it was illegal. Mecham said that was all he was doing. State officials said that his action cost the state an estimated $500 million in tourism, including the Super Bowl. The Arizona legislature in 1989 passed a state holiday honoring King, too late to win back the Super Bowl for 1993.

It did not take long for the new governor to perpetrate several highly publicized gaffes, such as defending use of the word "pickaninny," saying that Asian visitors' eyes become round when they see Arizona's golf courses, making insensitive remarks about Jews and gays, and pronouncing, "Well, the NBA, I guess they forget how many white people they get coming to watch them play."

Talk of a recall began two months after Mecham took office, but no effort to gather the required petition signatures could begin until he had been in office six months. The recall leader was Ed Buck, a thirty-three-year-old Phoenix businessman who was almost immediately attacked by Mecham supporters because he was gay. Mecham said he would welcome a recall. "At least a recall election I think would shut 'em all up. I'll tell you what, if a band of homosexuals and a few dissident Democrats can get me out of office, why heavens, the state deserves what else they can get."

Buck took out petitions on July 6, 1987, and eventually secured almost 350,000 signatures, twice as many as needed to force an election. The election was scheduled for May 17, 1988, and former Congressman John Rhodes agreed to run to replace Mecham. But before the election could be held, Mecham was impeached and removed from office.

He was impeached by the state house on February 5, 1988, in a vote of 46 to 14, on charges he had concealed a $350,000 campaign contribution, misused a state protocol fund by borrowing $80,000 to use at his Pontiac dealership, and obstructed justice by ordering the head of the state police to refuse to cooperate in a state investigation. He had been in office little more than a year. After a five-week trial, on April 4, 1988, the senate found Mecham guilty of high crimes and misdemeanors by a 26 to 4 vote. The action removed him from office.

He had also been criminally indicted on the campaign contribution charges but was acquitted in mid-June.

Mecham made another attempt to win the Republican nomination for governor in 1990, but he failed to raise enough money for his campaign. He had vowed that he would win the governor's chair again with the help of 10,000 members of a conservative "Mecham Militia." Phoenix businessman Fife Symington won the primary and then went on to capture the election in a three-way race.

Ten years after his impeachment, Mecham continued to defend his ways. In 1998 he self-published a 356-page book, *Wrong Impeachment,* in which he blamed his troubles on the state "power brokers," mostly the media and the Phoenix 40, a group of business interests. When he took office, he had promised to take power away from the "establishment."

"That promise made me a lot of powerful secret enemies," he said in the book's introduction, and soon after he took office, he was warned by sources that he would not be allowed to finish his term. "I underestimated both their determination to remove me, and their commitment to use any means, legal or not, foul or fair, to succeed."

Mecham claimed the assault was led by the *Arizona Republic,* which had "coordinated daily attacks on mostly phantom issues." He called the *Republic* the "Phoenix 40 propaganda machine" and called his opponent, Burton Barr, "the power brokers' errand boy." Regarding his impeachment, indictment, and recall, Mecham wrote: "No office holder in the history of the United States has ever been attacked simultaneously on those three fronts. . . . It pains me to say that Arizona is one of the most corrupt states in the Union."

He is now retired and living in Glendale.

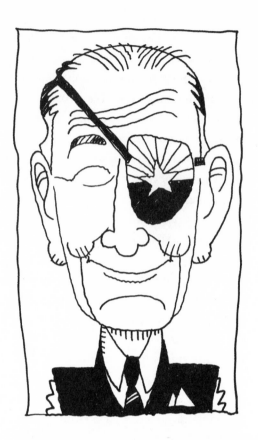

Lewis W. Douglas

One evening when he was ambassador to Great Britain, Lewis
Douglas was having a conversation with Winston Churchill and
Field Marshal Montgomery about their personal heroes. His hero,
Douglas said, was Jesus Garcia.

Puzzled looks came over Churchill and Montgomery. Who
was he?

Douglas explained that Garcia was a young railway engineer
who gave his life to save the Mexican town of Nacozari, Mexico.
He was driving a train loaded with explosives on November 7,

1907, between Nacozari and the Phelps Dodge Company mine, six miles away. The train caught fire, and Garcia piloted it away from Nacozari and died saving the town.

Douglas said he never forgot "this example of a person with a very high and deep-seated sense of responsibility so great he was prepared to face death." He became aware of the story because his grandfather, who was president of Phelps Dodge, dedicated a monument to Garcia in Nacozari.

But Lewis Douglas made a name for himself in his own right. He rose from the mining camps of Arizona to the halls of Congress to the Court of St. James's.

His grandfather was James Douglas, who invented a system for smelting copper that Phelps Dodge used at the Copper Queen Mine at Bisbee around 1878 to extract copper. James Douglas became head of Phelps Dodge, and the family put down roots in southeastern Arizona. He built a smelter to process ore from the Nacozari and Bisbee mines and established a town for workers nearby, which was named Douglas after him. His son, James S. "Rawhide Jimmy" Douglas, also entered the mining field, establishing the United Verde Extension Mine in Jerome and building a smelter in Clarkdale.

Lewis William Douglas was born on July 2, 1894, at his maternal grandparents' home in Bisbee. During his youth the mining town grew into a boisterous settlement of 8,000 people. At that time small bands of Apaches were in the area. Douglas said he remembered, as a child, being "chased by Indians, who harbored no kindly or generous intentions in their breasts, their minds, or their rifles."

At age eleven he was put on a train bound for the East, where he became a student at Hackley's School in Tarrytown, New York, then attended Montclair Military Academy in New Jersey. One Hackley instructor remembered that Douglas's "personality stood out from the others. Even as a boy he had about everything: emotional balance, ability to get along with boys and faculty, and a sense of humor that was hard to match." He was intelligent, but not the best of students.

Douglas entered Amherst in 1912, the year Arizona became a state. His studies improved at the Massachusetts school, and he graduated cum laude in 1916 with a degree in metallurgy and geology. He received a faculty award for outstanding scholarship and leadership.

Later he studied at the Massachusetts Institute of Technology but left to join the army as a lieutenant during World War I. Assigned to the 91st Division, one of the early units sent to France, he fought at Argonne, where he was wounded and gassed. He was cited for outstanding service by General John J. Pershing and decorated with Belgium's Croix de Guerre. After the war he taught history at Amherst for a year and studied law at Harvard.

In June 1921 he married Peggy Zinsser, whom he had met at a Smith-Amherst dance years earlier. They would have two boys and a girl, James Stuart, Lewis W. Jr., and Sharman. The couple headed west for Jerome, Arizona, where Lewis thought he would be an executive in his father's mine. His father had other ideas, putting him to work as a mucker at the 1,700-foot depths of the mine. The elder Douglas believed that his son should make his way through hard work, not by having a job handed to him. While working in the mine, an accident injured Douglas's eyes, so his father assigned him to collect miners' rents and settle their claims for damages. The miners liked Douglas, which led him to seek political office.

In 1922 Lewis Douglas was elected as a Democrat to the Arizona House of Representatives but left after one term to devote full time to his business enterprises, including citrus farming in the Salt River Valley. By 1927 his interest in politics was renewed, and he decided to run for Arizona's lone seat in the U.S. House of Representatives after the incumbent, Carl Hayden, announced he would run for the Senate. Accompanied by his wife,

Douglas campaigned in an old Ford, wearing a rumpled suit and battered old hat.

An editorial in one Arizona newspaper said of Douglas, "In the ordinary acceptance of the term, he is not a politician and there is no promise that he ever will be. He is too frank, straightforward and outspoken for that." Some editors said that he was trying to commit political suicide by his honesty, but others said the voters were tired of what one labeled "taffy, buncombe, and blatherskite."

He won the election and drew attention almost immediately in Congress. A nationally syndicated columnist described Douglas as a congressman who showed "a keen grasp of legislative questions and public problems, and he has a likeable personality. He is handsome, wealthy, personable and intelligent; it seems that all the good fairies were present at his birth." He was rumored to be in line for a cabinet post, perhaps as head of the State, Treasury, or War Department in the new Roosevelt administration.

After Douglas had served three terms as Arizona's congressman, Roosevelt selected him as his budget director, an office he assumed on March 4, 1933. The New York Herald Tribune said he had "shown that he has the sort of two-fisted courage which not only enables a man to stand for the right but to make that right prevail." The humorist Will Rogers, noting that Douglas was the only congressman from Arizona, mused, "Every state ought to have only one. Arizona does better with one than New York does with forty-five." Vice President John Nance Garner praised Douglas's courage: "In fact, he has got so much courage that he voted with the Democrats about half the time he was in the House and the rest of the time he didn't. That's courage." It was that kind of voting record that led others to wonder through the years whether he had more Republican tendencies than Democratic.

As a fiscal conservative, Douglas opposed deficit spending. In a letter to his father, he complained that Roosevelt's spending programs were "mad and reckless." Finally, after eighteen months as budget director, Roosevelt's pump-priming fiscal policies prompted him to resign. He said the president's policy of deliberate, excessive spending would produce a recovery "as empty as a blown-out eggshell." Roosevelt asked him to delay his resignation until after the congressional elections, saying he felt that Douglas's departure would cost him Democratic seats in Congress. Douglas refused, saying it would be dishonest.

Whereas earlier Vice President Garner had praised him, now he attacked him for his alleged disloyalty to the Democrats. Douglas was not bothered because he had done what he thought was best for his country. He believed that his first loyalty was to his country, the second to his state, and the third to his party. "Whenever these three conflict," he said, "[I] resolve the conflict in favor of the higher loyalty. This, I believe, is the essence of being a good Democrat, and this, I believe, is the essence of being a good American."

Several months after leaving office, Douglas continued his attack on Roosevelt's New Deal, saying there was a "deadly parallel" between New Deal fiscal policies and Soviet reforms after the fall of the czar. He later attacked the New Deal in his book *The Liberal Tradition*, but the *New York Herald Tribune* criticized him for his "hysterical gloom, his violent antagonism to everything represented in the New Deal, and his nervous extremism."

After he left the Roosevelt administration, Douglas thought about running to replace Isabella Greenway in the House but decided against it because of his conflicts with the Roosevelt administration. Instead, he returned to the private sector, serving as a vice president of the American Cyanamid Company from 1934 to 1938, then principal and vice chancellor of McGill University in Montreal from 1938 to 1940. He was the first U.S. citizen to hold the latter post, which he accepted only after his father promised him a stipend of $25,000 a year to assuage his worries about the financial hardship the job's paltry salary would impose. His major accomplishment at McGill was helping restore the university to financial well-being after years of deficit spending.

In 1940 Douglas was ready to return to the United States but rejected academic positions because they paid too little for his high lifestyle. He decided instead to become president of the Mutual Life Insurance Company of New York for $75,000 a year, holding the position from 1940 to 1947. It was wartime, so he also took on the job of administering the lend-lease program to Britain and was a deputy war shipping administrator.

In 1947 Douglas received a telephone call one night while having dinner. It was from Secretary of State George C. Marshall, asking him to become ambassador to the Court of St. James's. The *New York Times* remarked that "Truman could not possibly have chosen a better man." It was from that post that he helped institute the Marshall Plan, a strategy to rejuvenate war-torn Europe. During his tenure as ambassador, he earned the respect of the British people for his knowledge, his tact and charm, and his strong belief in Anglo-American cooperation. Disarmingly engaging, he also won over the British press. As his secretary wrote soon after their arrival in London, "[Douglas] has an air of simplicity and utter genuineness that has completely captivated the local newspaper boys."

As ambassador, he needed considerable charm. He was generally well groomed and impeccably dressed. He had little interest in food and would have eaten "nails with ketchup" if it were served to him, according to his biographers, Robert Paul Browder and Thomas G. Smith. He enjoyed good wine, drank vodka, and smoked in his younger years. His secretaries referred to him as "the late Mr. Douglas" because he was continually tardy. He was known for his independence and his integrity.

An eye injury that occurred while he was fly fishing for

salmon in England in April 1949 was the chief reason for his resignation as ambassador in 1950. He was casting when a gust of wind blew the fly back and it hooked in his left eye. For many years thereafter he wore a black patch over the eye. The wife of the president of Hathaway shirts was impressed with the distinction the patch gave Douglas and persuaded her husband to use the idea in advertising his product. The first advertisements appeared in 1951, using a model who resembled Douglas. They were an instant success.

When his eye continued to bother him, Douglas agreed to take his doctors' advice to rest, hoping that a "return to the sunlight of Arizona [would] dispel the constant pain in this eye." News of his resignation was met with universal regret. Sir Arthur Salter, who had been head of the British Merchant Shipping Commission to Washington during the war, said of Douglas, "Few Ambassadors have left this country amid such general and sincere expressions of regret and admiration as Mr. Lewis Douglas, and no Ambassador's wife and daughter have acquired such popularity and affection." Anthony Eden, who would later become prime minister, said Douglas "will hold a special place in history as the man whose skill as the interpreter between two great nations has nourished understanding at a critical hour." In 1957 Queen Elizabeth would bestow on him the honorary Grand Cross of the Order of the British Empire, one of Britain's highest honors.

During his term Douglas lived at 14 Prince's Gate, South Kensington, where he often was visited by Princess Elizabeth and Princess Margaret. One evening Elizabeth, now queen, dropped in to learn to play canasta, which the ambassador taught her with his glasses perched on his brow, like a schoolteacher.

In 1951 he returned to Douglas, where he became chairman of the board of Southern Arizona Bank and Trust Company. Economically and politically conservative, he found himself a minority in the Democratic Party. He rarely voted for a Democrat for president after 1932 and supported Barry Goldwater for the Senate in 1952 and 1958. He even voted for New York Governor Tom Dewey for president against Truman. Although he did not formally endorse General Dwight D. Eisenhower in 1952, he let it be known he favored him over Adlai Stevenson. Later he became a deputy economic adviser to Secretary of State John Foster Dulles in the Eisenhower administration.

In the 1960s and early 1970s, Douglas retired to his 15,000-acre ranch near Sonoita. He had purchased it in 1945 and formed the Douglas Livestock Company, realizing a lifelong dream to become an Arizona rancher. There he played host to countless dignitaries, including Princess Margaret and her husband, the Earl of Snowden, in 1965.

He fulfilled one act of final public service by agreeing, at Secretary of the Interior Stewart Udall's request, to serve on a presidential task force in 1966–67 concerning policy toward Native Americans. The final report urged a search for new ways to lead Native Americans to "equal citizenship, maximum self-sufficiency and full participating in American lives."

At the beginning of the new year 1974, Douglas took ill while staying with friends in New York. Surgery for an intestinal obstruction weakened his already frail health, and after more than two weeks of hospitalization, physicians saw little hope for recovery. His wife flew him home to die.

Douglas once told newspaperman William Allen White that Arizona "is a beautiful country, and its people are nice people. Their point of view, I think, is my point of view because I was born and raised there. They are, as it were, a part of me. Their country is my country. . . . I shall go [there] during the closing days of my life, if I can anticipate sufficiently the coming of the end."

He was able to spend his last days on his beloved ranch, dying on March 7, 1974, at the age of eighty.

Sandra Day O'Connor

Her early days on an Arizona ranch evoke comparisons to a life out of *Little House on the Prairie* or to Annie Oakley, but what Sandra Day O'Connor has accomplished far outstrips those classic stories of the frontier, fictional or otherwise. Her place in history is assured as the first woman to serve on the U.S. Supreme Court, an appointment that drew praise and criticism from the moment she was nominated by President Reagan in 1981.

"Being the first woman justice of the Supreme Court is very important to me," she said at the time, "but what is most important is that I am a good judge. We're all here, in part, to help others and to try to leave this place better than we found it. I have always thought that being a judge is one way to help others."

Although it is unlikely she would have been appointed had she been a man—her judicial record was rather undistinguished—being the first woman on the Court has cast her as a role model. "She exemplifies the notion that a person, a woman, can be professional and strong without being strident," says Arizona Supreme Court Justice Ruth McGregor. "She is able to be sure of herself without being arrogant or condescending."

Sandra Day O'Connor was born on March 26, 1930, in El Paso, Texas. Her parents, Harry and Ada Mae Day, owned a 198,000-acre cattle ranch called the Lazy B, which had been established by her grandfather Henry Clay Day in the 1880s near Duncan, Arizona. She grew up learning to ride horses, rope steers, round up cattle, and drive a tractor. She could fix windmills and repair fences. "My friends and I played with dolls, but we knew what to do with screwdrivers and nails, too. Even now, I'm a pretty good shot with a rifle." She has said that she used to "get up at 3:00 A.M. and be in the saddle by sunup."

The family ranch house was a simple four-room adobe building that had no electricity or running water until Sandra was seven. Her days were spent mostly in isolation, as the nearest neighbors lived twenty-five miles away. An only child until she was eight years old, she befriended the ranch's cowboys and kept many pets, including a bobcat. She once napped on a case of dynamite behind the backseat of an old car. Her mother spent hours reading to her from the *Wall Street Journal, Los Angeles Times, New Yorker,* and *Saturday Evening Post.* The ranch provided a sanctuary when she wanted to escape until it was sold in 1986.

The isolation of the ranch made formal education difficult, so Sandra's parents sent her to live with her maternal grandmother in El Paso. She attended the Radford School in El Paso, a private academy for girls, and then Austin High School, graduating with good marks at the age of sixteen.

Her education continued at Stanford University, where she majored in economics to prepare herself to operate her own ranch or the Lazy B. But a legal dispute over her family's ranch prompted an interest in law, and Sandra Day became the first woman to enroll at Stanford Law School after graduating magna cum laude in 1950.

A brilliant student, she took only two years instead of the customary three to complete law school and garnered such honors as editorship of the *Stanford Law Review* and membership in the Order of the Coif, a legal honor society. At Stanford Law she also met her future husband, John Jay O'Connor, and graduated with William H. Rehnquist, who would become chief justice of the United States.

Law firms were reluctant to hire women lawyers in the early 1950s, and the only job she was offered was as a legal secretary, which she declined. "I couldn't imagine not getting work in what I trained for," she says. The secretarial offer came from a firm in which a senior partner was William French Smith, who almost thirty years later would help push through O'Connor's nomination to the Supreme Court when he was President Reagan's attorney general. When Smith notified her that she was being nominated, O'Connor joked, "Oh, I guess you must mean in a secretarial position."

Like other women who found themselves in a man's world, O'Connor turned to the government rather than work as a secretary, accepting a job as a deputy county attorney in San Mateo, California. Today she recalls how that job "influenced the balance of my life because it demonstrated how much I did enjoy public service."

When John O'Connor graduated from Stanford a year later, the army drafted him into the Judge Advocate General Corps.

He was stationed for three years in Frankfurt, Germany, where Sandra served as a civilian lawyer in the Quartermaster's Corps.

The O'Connors returned to the United States in 1957 and settled in Phoenix because its size and growth offered better opportunities. Sandra again found it difficult to obtain a position with any law firm, so she started her own with a single partner, working from an office that was wedged between a TV store and a laundry. As a virtually unknown lawyer, she handled a wide variety of small cases before taking off five years during the time her three sons, Scott, Brian, and Jay, were born. "Two things were clear to me from the onset," O'Connor has remarked. "One was, I wanted a family and the second was that I wanted to work—and I love to work."

While raising her sons, she became involved in volunteer activities, devoting time to the Arizona State Hospital, the Arizona State Bar, the Salvation Army, and local schools. She also participated in Republican politics. When she returned to work in 1965, it was as an assistant Arizona attorney general.

O'Connor got her break in politics when Republican Governor Jack Williams appointed her to a vacant state senate seat in 1969. She ran successfully for two more terms and eventually became the majority leader, a first for a woman in the United States. As a state senator, she surprised Republicans by supporting the proposed Equal Rights Amendment and casting several pro-abortion votes. She also was a supporter of legislation requiring open meetings of public agencies.

O'Connor was establishing herself as one of Arizona's outspoken advocates for women. Among other actions, she sponsored repeal of an old Arizona law that limited women to working eight hours a day. Overall, her voting record ranged from moderate to conservative. She opposed the death penalty, fought gun control, and opposed busing as a way to end segregation. Her pro-abortion stand in the legislature raised and continues to raise questions. In defense of her votes, she has stated, "My own view in the area of abortion is that I am opposed to it as a matter of birth control or otherwise."

"She's finished at the top in a lot of things," says Mary Ellen Simonson of Phoenix, who was a legislative aide when O'Connor was state senate majority leader. "She has a reputation for excelling. As a result, she's been one of the state's leading role models for women."

In 1974 O'Connor was elected to a seat on the Maricopa County Superior Court bench. State Republican leaders urged her to run for governor in 1978, but she declined. A year later the new Democratic governor, Bruce Babbitt, appointed her to the Arizona Court of Appeals. The Arizona State Bar had given her an 85 percent rating as a superior court judge and a 90 percent rating on the appellate court.

McGregor remembers learning a lot from the year she spent in 1981 clerking for O'Connor. "She has unbelievable organizational skills," she says. "I've never in my life known anyone who is as capable as she is in compressing so many things in one day and doing them all well."

A turning point came in 1976 when O'Connor backed Ronald Reagan in his losing effort to gain the Republican nomination over Gerald Ford. After Reagan was elected president in 1980, he returned the favor by fulfilling a campaign promise to appoint a woman to the Supreme Court. Although it probably helped that she had a close relationship with Rehnquist dating back to their days at Stanford, it wasn't the strongest of endorsements, and she was burdened with greater expectations.

"Without doubt," Reagan said at the time, "the most awesome appointment a president can make is to the United States Supreme Court." Recalling his campaign promise, he added, "That is not to say I would appoint a woman merely to do so. That would not be fair to women, nor to future generations of all Americans whose lives are so deeply affected by decisions of the court. Rather, I pledged to appoint a woman who meets the very high standards I demand of all court appointees."

O'Connor's nomination was quick to draw criticism from both the left and the right. It drew praise from such diverse senators as Republican Barry Goldwater and Democrat Ted Kennedy. Liberals could not deny their satisfaction at seeing a woman nominated to the high court, but they were dismayed at O'Connor's apparent lack of strong support for feminist issues. Conservatives, on the other hand, derided her lack of federal judicial experience and claimed she came up short in constitutional knowledge. They considered her a wasted nomination and thought her position on abortion was suspect.

Evangelist Jerry Falwell in particular was upset with her stand on abortion. That led to one of the classic exchanges between Arizonans Goldwater and Morris Udall. When Udall read Goldwater's remark that Christians should line up to kick Falwell in the ass, he tore the article out of the newspaper and sent it to Goldwater with the following note: "That's a good idea, but it wouldn't accomplish anything because Falwell is a good Christian and he would simply turn the other cheek."

Udall, a Democrat, rallied to O'Connor's aid. "She has good judicial temperament," he said. "She can be tough. She clearly is a conservative, but she has never placed partisan political values before justice. Those who practice in her court describe her as practical, conscientious, fair, and open-minded. . . . My Democratic friends ought to be grateful for this appointment. It's almost inconceivable to me that they could do any better."

O'Connor's three-day confirmation hearings attracted a record number of journalists, witnesses, and spectators. In her opening statement she said, "As the first woman to be nominated as a Supreme Court justice, I am particularly honored, but I happily share the honor with millions of American women of yesterday and today whose abilities and conduct have given me this opportunity for service."

She calmly discussed her beliefs about the law, stating that, in her opinion, "judges should avoid substituting their own views . . . for those of the legislature." Elected legislators, she maintained, are more "attuned to the public will" and more "politically accountable" than appointed judges. She also recounted some of the prejudices she had encountered as a newly graduated female lawyer in the 1950s.

She steadfastly refused to predict how she would vote as a Supreme Court justice, particularly on the politically sensitive issue of abortion. When asked how she wanted to be remembered, O'Connor replied: "Ah, the tombstone question. I hope it says, 'Here lies a good judge.' " O'Connor won the approval of seventeen of the Senate Judiciary Committee's eighteen members. A few days later the full Senate confirmed her as an associate justice of the Supreme Court by a vote of 99 to 0.

After she was sworn in on September 25, 1981, as the 102nd Supreme Court justice, she began her long workdays, often seven days a week. During her first days on the Court, stacks of handwritten letters came to her desk, most from women pleased to know that one of their own had attained power. For several years, until Madeleine Albright became secretary of state in the Clinton administration, she was considered the most powerful woman in the country. Talk abounded that if Bob Dole had been elected president in 1996 and Rehnquist had retired, she would have become chief justice.

In the fall of 1988, O'Connor was diagnosed with breast cancer. The day before her surgery, she fulfilled a speaking engagement at Washington and Lee University, and she was back on the bench ten days afterward, without missing an oral argument. She didn't tell her brother and sister about her cancer until after the surgery. "She never once cried on my shoulder," Alan Day said. There were rumors she would resign or ease up on her rigorous schedule. "Out of the question," her sister, Ann, said. "No one at the Court works harder and gets more mileage out of a day than she does."

In her early years as a justice, O'Connor was considered very conservative. During her first year she voted with Chief Justice Warren Burger and Rehnquist on sixty-two of eighty-four opinions and opposed them only five times. Out of 137 cases, she voted with Rehnquist on 123. *Time* magazine labeled her Rehnquist's "Arizona twin"; indeed, in her first term the two voted together on twenty-seven of the thirty-one decisions decided by 5 to 4 votes. The reference to Arizona twin irked her, and she began to pull away from Rehnquist.

In subsequent terms O'Connor often voted with centrist Lewis F. Powell, Jr., and the two were in the majority on 5 to 4 rulings more often than any other justices. While O'Connor generally sided with her conservative colleagues, she frequently wrote her own, narrower concurrence. Over the first ten years on the Court, she was found more supportive of criminal defendants and civil rights than Rehnquist.

O'Connor often became the swing vote on a Court sharply divided over such issues as affirmative action, the death penalty, and abortion. "As O'Connor goes, so goes the Court," one observer said in 1990. When David Souter joined the Court that fall, he and she voted the same way in every 5 to 4 decision during his first term.

Legal scholars often are puzzled by her shifts in judicial decisions. While often conservative, her decisions also are open-minded, reflecting no profound ideology and devoid of rhetoric. Critics say that her opinions lack passion, vision, and a personal tone.

O'Connor has been compared to Justices Powell and John Marshall Harlan, "whose careers were distinguished by a devotion to pragmatic resolution of the issues before them." She is described as a justice "who looks to resolve each case and no more, one with no overarching philosophy that might pre-ordain a result."

Thurgood Marshall once said about O'Connor, "History will judge all of us, and Sandra will do a lot better by history than most of us."

Rachael Pine, a senior litigator with the Center for Re-productive Law and Policy in New York City, has said: "If we could have a court full of O'Connors, nine justices who don't give you a knee-jerk response but who try to calculate the truth as they find it, then you could say the system is working the way it is supposed to work."

On October 23, 2000, the $84 million, 500,000-square-foot federal courthouse at 401 West Washington Street, in Phoe-nix, Arizona, was dedicated in her honor.

In early 2001, not long after the George W. Bush admin-istration took power, rumors abounded that O'Connor might retire so that a Republican president could appoint a new justice. She responded that it was "just not true. . . . I have no present plan to retire." Her health is good and she is leading a vigorous life. She is good enough on the golf course to have hit a hole-in-one in 2000 at the Paradise Valley Golf Course in Arizona.

She and her brother wrote a book about the family ranch in Duncan. Entitled *Lazy B: Growing Up on a Cattle Ranch in the American Southwest,* it was published by Random House in Janu-ary 2002.

Ernest McFarland

Ernest W. McFarland is the only politician in Arizona—perhaps in the United States—to have served in the highest office of each branch of government. He was a U.S. senator, governor, and chief justice of the Arizona Supreme Court.

His place in history may be secure for having achieved the triple crown of politics, but one other accomplishment that is less well known had an enormous impact on the well-being of the United States during the second half of the twentieth century. McFarland was the primary sponsor of the G.I. Bill after World

War II, which enabled tens of thousands of veterans to get a college education and become productive members of society.

He once said his philosophy of life was, "If you want to get ahead in life, you either need to be smarter than the average person or willing to work harder than the average person." He said he had seen those who thought they were smarter than anyone else fail and so he worked hard so he wouldn't fail.

Ernest William McFarland was born in a one-room cabin on October 9, 1894, near the town of Earlsboro, Oklahoma. His parents had settled in the Pottawatomie Strip in 1891 soon after it was opened. Mac, as he was commonly called, graduated third in a class of three at Earlsboro High School and earned a two-year teaching certificate at East Central Normal School, later to become East Central State College. He taught in a one-room schoolhouse in the small town of Schoolton, Oklahoma, before enrolling at the University of Oklahoma to get his bachelor's degree.

When World War I broke out, he joined the navy. After being discharged, he headed to Arizona, a state he had heard "quite a bit about." Arriving in Phoenix with ten dollars in his pocket, he went to an employment agency for ex-servicemen and got a job as a teller in a nearby bank. But banking was not for him, and he quit to attend law school at Stanford University. Before he left, he filed a homesteading claim for 160 acres near Casa Grande, Arizona, which he called his "jackrabbit farm."

While attending law school, he met a fellow student, Clare Collins, whom he married in 1925, but theirs was a short, tragic union. Their two children died shortly after they were born, and his wife died in 1930, apparently depressed over their deaths.

After law school McFarland returned to Arizona and set up a law practice in Casa Grande. Times were hard, with little or no work available in the law, so he dabbled in politics during the 1922 election, hoping to land some work after the election. His plan was successful, and he got a job as an assistant attorney general for the state. Two years later he was elected Pinal County attorney and served six years. Then, in 1930, he ran as a Democrat for superior court judge in Pinal County but lost the election by eighty votes to the sitting judge, E. L. Green, and returned to private practice.

One of his cases was a particularly famous one, representing the notorious trunk murderer Winnie Ruth Judd. She had killed her two roommates, dismembered their bodies, and hauled them in a suitcase to Los Angeles. McFarland's insanity defense saved Judd from the death penalty. She escaped seven times from the state mental hospital but was always recaptured and returned to the hospital. Ever grateful to her lawyer, Judd promised not to give him trouble when he was elected governor. She made good on her word, never making an escape attempt during his term.

McFarland ran for judge again in 1934, this time without opposition. During his court tenure he married a mathematics and history teacher, Edna Eveland Smith, with whom he had a daughter, Jewell. After serving six years on the bench, he ran against the redoubtable Henry Ashurst, who had been U.S. senator for Arizona's twenty-eight years of statehood. Ashurst, believing he was unbeatable, rarely returned to Arizona to campaign. McFarland took advantage of that and surprised Ashurst with an almost 2 to 1 margin of victory.

McFarland arrived in Washington in 1941 and was assigned to the Senate committees on Indian Affairs, Interstate Commerce, Irrigation and Reclamation, Judiciary, and Pensions. Not long after joining the Senate, he was appointed to a special committee to investigate the motion picture and radio industries on charges of propaganda. McFarland wrote in his autobiography that newspapers said he had been appointed because he could be "counted on to be a mere figurehead—nontroublesome window dressing." But he proved critics wrong, defending the industries and noting that critics had not even seen the suspect movies. He received national publicity for his efforts, and nothing came of the investigation. McFarland also served on a communications subcommittee that sparked his interest in communications and led him to form the Arizona Television Company, channel 3 in Phoenix, which went on the air on March 1, 1955.

McFarland called passage of the G.I. Bill one of the most important events in his Senate career. He had seen many veterans who could not find jobs after World War I, and he wanted to prevent the same thing happening after World War II. His legislation assured financial assistance to returning veterans.

In 1950, during the Truman administration, McFarland was chosen Senate majority leader and appointed Lyndon Johnson as his majority whip. He had become good friends with Truman during the president's tenure in the Senate, and their relationship continued when Truman moved to the White House. McFarland believed that it was important to relay the Senate's views, good or bad, to the president.

"I never hesitated to present views contrary to those of the president in our conferences," he said. "As I've said before, I think that too frequently, the president is only told things people think he wants to hear. I would like to emphasize that it is not pleasant to present a view contrary to that of the president in such conferences."

In the 1952 election McFarland seems to have fallen victim to the same misjudgment Ashurst made when McFarland ran against him. He was immensely popular and held a position of leadership in the Senate, and Arizona was overwhelmingly Democratic. Nevertheless, a brash, upstart Republican member of the Phoenix City Council decided to challenge him.

McFarland appeared unconcerned about Barry Goldwater, an inexperienced though highly charismatic newcomer to politics. Goldwater asked voters to choose between "fear and faith." He attacked Truman's record and never let voters forget that McFarland was a Truman man. Like Ashurst, McFarland did too little campaigning, choosing to remain in Washington to tend to business.

A McFarland adviser after the election blamed McFarland's loss in part on the Burma Shave–like signs that Goldwater had strung along the state's highways. Posted at 100-foot intervals, one line to each eight-inch by four-foot sign, they said: "Mac is for Harry. Harry's all through. You be for Barry. 'Cause Barry's for you." The final sign said, "Goldwater for Senate."

Goldwater rarely mentioned McFarland's name in speeches, referring to him as the junior senator. His tactic was to attack the Truman administration while linking himself to General Dwight D. Eisenhower's presidential campaign. McFarland had boasted that he was one of the four most powerful men in Washington, and Goldwater turned that against him, blaming him for everything from the stalemate in the Korean War to tax increases.

Goldwater particularly seized on a statement McFarland made about the Korean War while speaking to a friendly service club in Coolidge, Arizona. McFarland called it a cheap war because the United States was killing nine Chinese for every American. He also said the war was making the United States prosperous. Goldwater's campaign director, Stephen Shadegg, said Goldwater's attack on that statement may have swung the election in his favor. Goldwater defeated McFarland by 6,725 votes out of a total of about 260,000. Eisenhower carried Arizona by 44,000 votes, and linking himself to Eisenhower helped Goldwater.

In his self-published autobiography, McFarland mentioned nothing about that race against Goldwater in 1952. That omission showed the depth of McFarland's bitterness over his loss to Goldwater.

Two years after this defeat, McFarland was elected governor, beating Republican incumbent Howard Pyle by 12,238 votes even though polls showed that Pyle would win by 15,000. A Republican analysis of the race indicated that Pyle lost the race rather than McFarland winning it. Pyle was criticized for assembling a task force of 250 men who moved into Short Creek, a tiny

Mormon settlement in northern Arizona, where polygamy was being illegally practiced. The show of power and the fact that none of the polygamists were found guilty of more than a misdemeanor backfired against Pyle. Even the Republican newspaper, the *Arizona Republic,* called it an artificially created script right out of Hollywood.

McFarland's administration was marked by such accomplishments as improving the state's economic climate, bringing water to arid Arizona, and improving the state's three public universities. One of his great unrealized dreams was to establish a seaport in the southwest corner of the state that would give Arizona access to the Gulf of Mexico. It also was during his administration that a decision was reached to build the Glen Canyon Dam, situating it just south of the Utah border in Arizona. That led to establishment of the town of Page in Arizona. In reflection, even the Republican Party agreed that McFarland had done a good job.

In 1954 a radio commentator, Jack Williams, a Republican who later became governor, said about McFarland: "He may not be smart, but he's governor. He may not be smart, but he has been U.S. senator, and a lot of the smart ones can't say either. . . . If he isn't smart, I'd like to be whatever he is—even if you just call him lucky."

He was reelected again in 1956, beating Horace Griffen by 171,848 votes to 116,744, the biggest margin for any state or national candidate in Arizona history. But he let it be known that he would not seek a third term and that he would challenge Goldwater in 1958. He was extremely bitter about his defeat in 1952.

During his second two-year term, McFarland established the State Parks and Recreation Board to protect the natural landscapes and wildlife in Arizona. He campaigned for taxes on tobacco, alcohol, and fuel to help fund education and road improvements, and he persuaded the legislature to reduce the six-day work week for state employees to five.

"The work that I enjoyed the most [as governor] really was trying to help the youth of our state," he wrote in his autobiography. "I was interested in the young people. As governor you can't do everything that you want to do. You don't accomplish everything. But if you can build a little bit for the youth I think that's more important than building a highway—and we built plenty of highways."

He lost his second race against Goldwater. Once again in his autobiography, he gave little attention to the race but remarked that it was "a bitter and hard-fought one." He left the impression that his opponent ran a dirty campaign. Goldwater released information claiming that McFarland had accepted illegal campaign contributions from the labor movement. At the end of the exhausting campaign, voters returned Goldwater to the Senate by a 35,000-vote margin.

McFarland returned to private law practice until 1964, when he set out to fulfill a lifelong dream of serving on the state supreme court—at the age of seventy. "This was a position I had considered one of the highest in our government," he said, "but also one which I had never really expected to attain. . . . It was an opportunity to round out my governmental work in my profession." Of all the titles—senator, governor, judge—he preferred to be addressed as judge the rest of his life.

In those days justices were elected. He won with 60 percent of the vote and served from 1965 to 1971. One of the most controversial cases to come before the court while McFarland was serving was the Miranda case, which centered on the rights of the accused. McFarland wrote the opinion that upheld the abduction and rape conviction of Miranda, who claimed his right to an attorney had been violated. McFarland said that Miranda was familiar with the criminal justice system and that he had volunteered his confession and did not ask for an attorney. The conviction was later overturned by the U.S. Supreme Court, which ruled that a defendant had to be notified of the right to an attorney.

McFarland wrote more than three hundred opinions during his six years on the bench. Once when they were traveling by plane, Supreme Court Justice Fred Struckmeyer, Jr., asked McFarland why he was working on files rather than relaxing. Later he related, "At 30,000 feet, there was nothing to see out the window, the magazines were out of date, and I was too old to stare at the stewardesses."

When McFarland retired, Charles J. Meyers, dean of the law school at Stanford University, where he had earned his law degree, said, "His well-reasoned opinions, personal integrity, and years of exemplary public service have set standards for all judges, lawyers, and politicians to aspire to."

In retirement he became president of KTVK television in Phoenix, the station he had founded in 1955.

In 1974 he purchased the old Pinal County Court House in Florence. Built in 1878, the old adobe building had been condemned and was scheduled for demolition. He transferred the deed to the State Parks Board, and the McFarlands established a trust fund for its reconstruction. Later it became part of McFarland State Park. The courthouse houses his papers and memorabilia.

McFarland told historians Abe and Mildred Chanin that in his earlier days in politics, he'd had "a lot of dreams that you don't expect to realize. I never expected to do all the things that I've done." He died on June 8, 1984, in Phoenix.

George W.P. Hunt

He called himself "the Old Walrus," and at five-feet-nine, weighing almost 300 pounds, with a bald head and a huge handle-bar mustache, Arizona's first governor, George W.P. Hunt, certainly fit the description. Dressed in a white linen suit that was often spotted with chewing tobacco juice, he could be crusty and uncouth.

Nevertheless, Arizonans liked their colorful chief executive, electing him to seven two-year terms after statehood in 1912. He was a Progressive and a humanitarian, as well as an ardent friend of labor, probably because of his early mining days.

"He is too astute a politician to ever break a promise once made, but he is too good a philosopher ever to make a promise," said Frank C. Lockwood, a liberal arts dean at the University of Arizona, in his book *Arizona Characters*.

His life's motto was "Remember your friends, and forget your enemies."

In late 1881, at the age of twenty-two, Hunt wandered into Globe, Arizona, wearing overalls and leading a burro after walking across country. He would call Globe his home the rest of his life.

George Wylley Paul Hunt was born on November 1, 1859, in Huntsville, Missouri, a town named for his grandfather. His family had lost everything during the Civil War, and he grew up poor, once failing a class because he could not afford a book. That experience led him to champion free books for students in Arizona public schools when he was governor.

He ran away from home at the age of eighteen in 1878 because his mother wanted him to become a doctor. He worked his way across the country washing dishes and serving meals in restaurants and wound up in Arizona's White Mountains, where he prospected from Springerville to Safford before ending up in Globe.

He tried his hand as a mucker in the Old Dominion Mine, as a ranch hand, and in a variety of other odd jobs. When he was thirty-one years old, he got a job as a delivery boy with A. Bailey and Company, a general store, and moved steadily up the chain of command over a ten-year period. When the company was merged into the Old Dominion Commercial Company, he became its president and was able to live a financially comfortable life.

Hunt's first try at public office came in 1890, when he ran unsuccessfully for Gila County recorder. Two years later he won a seat in the territorial house of representatives. He then worked for a brief period as Gila County treasurer before being elected to the legislature, where he served from 1895 to 1898. Then he dropped out of politics for the next six years. During his terms in office, he supported women's right to vote, income tax, secret ballots, and compulsory schooling.

On February 24, 1904, Hunt married Helen Duett Ellison, who had been raised on a ranch in Gila County. They had one daughter, Virginia. His wife ran the general store while Hunt was off pursuing politics.

He was a delegate to the 1900 Democratic convention in Kansas City when William Jennings Bryan was nominated for president. He returned to the territorial legislature in 1905 and was elected its president, serving in that post until statehood in 1912. Afterward, he served as president of the constitution convention, which wrote the state constitution over a two-month period. Among the members of the body were the grandfathers of Stewart and Mo Udall and Barry Goldwater. When Hunt expressed his support of the Progressive movement, he drew criticism from those who believed in the status quo; they labeled him a socialist. Undeterred, he denounced entrenched wealth and "big interests."

In becoming the first governor of Arizona, Democrat Hunt beat Republican Judge Edmund W. Wells of Prescott in a close race. The new state legislature met in March to revise the territorial code. Among Hunt's legislative initiatives were anti–child labor laws, an anti-usury law, a law that would require newspapers to disclose their stockholders, an anti-lobbying law, and old-age pension and workers' compensation laws. At one point during his governorship, he proposed a unicameral, or single-chamber, legislature, but the idea went nowhere. Nebraska is the only state with a unicameral legislature.

Hunt ran for governor eight times between 1911 and 1932, winning six times by ballot, one time when courts declared him the winner, and losing one time. He enjoyed the patronage that came with the governorship, rewarding his friends with highway jobs and never letting them forget it. He was supported by organized labor and often carried on a running feud with what he called the "special interests and their mouthpieces, the daily press." Because of his association with the Industrial Workers of the World, he was linked to America's enemies during World War I. One Flagstaff resident challenged his loyalty to the country. Hunt sued and collected one cent in damages.

When Hunt lost his reelection bid to Republican Thomas Campbell, he refused to give up the office, demanding a recount. On December 30, 1916, he and Campbell both took the oath. Hunt vacated the seat on January 27, 1917, but was reinstated on Christmas day when the state supreme court declared him the victor by forty-two votes.

In 1918 he decided against running again, saying that he was exhausted by the burdens of the office. But by mid-1919 he was bored and announced he would challenge Marcus Aurelius Smith for his U.S. Senate seat. It seems that Smith may have outfoxed him. As legend has it, Smith got together with the other Democratic senator, Henry Ashurst, to ask President Woodrow Wilson to appoint Hunt to a diplomatic post to get him out of Arizona. When Smith and Ashurst met with Wilson, the president supposedly turned a globe upside down, put his finger on a spot, and asked, "Would this be far enough?" Wilson then appointed Hunt minister to Siam.

Hunt took the ministry, but he knew how it had been set up. So while in Bangkok, he sent postcards to the majority of Arizona's voters. When he returned from the tour in 1921, he had trunkloads of souvenirs that he handed out to his faithful supporters. In 1922 he ran again for governor, this time against the man who had replaced him, Tom Campbell, and won. Each time he was elected, he would become George the V, then George the VI, and so on.

One of Hunt's positions in the 1922 race set back Arizona's

efforts to attain its fair share of Colorado River water, which was finally decided by the U.S. Supreme Court in 1964. Because Campbell supported the Colorado River Compact, which would have established that share, Hunt opposed it, and the compact was not signed until 1944. The delay forced the state to enter into costly litigation to acquire its share.

Hunt opposed capital punishment, but when the voters decided to restore executions, he did not veto the law. He was a staunch ally of prison reform and even had a spare room in the warden's quarters at the state penitentiary in Florence, where he would stay whenever he came to the prison to meet with inmates.

The governor was reelected in 1924 and 1926. When he ran in 1928 at the age of almost seventy, he met Will Rogers at the airport. Rogers asked him how his "hereditary governorship" was going and wondered whether Hunt might adopt him so he could succeed him. But Hunt lost that race to John C. Phillips in the Hoover landslide of 1928.

Then the Great Depression set in, and it took little coaxing to get Hunt back to seek reelection. He narrowly defeated Phillips and was sworn in for what would be his last term. By 1932 the Republicans had had enough of Hunt and his populism.

Arizona actually had two Democratic parties: the Hunt party and the anti-Hunt party. The Republicans made up about a third of the populace. Many of them registered as Democrats so they could vote against Hunt in the primary. The strategy worked, and Hunt was defeated by Benjamin Baker Moeur in 1932, one of three Democrats to challenge him in the primary. Moeur went on to become governor. Hunt ran again in the Democratic primary in 1934 but lost again to Moeur, ending his political career. He had hoped to land a position with the Roosevelt administration, but that never came to be.

Hunt was nothing if not flamboyant, and his quirkiness, along with his populist sympathies, no doubt endeared him to his constituents. During World War I the governor knitted scarves for soldiers and said he wished he could join the marines, even though he was almost sixty. Once on an official state visit to a Mormon colony of polygamists along the Arizona-Utah border, he reputedly remarked, "Hell, if I had to live in this place, I'd want more than one wife myself." He disliked parades and ceremonies. During a campaign an aide asked him to let him know when he was coming to Tucson so he could have a band meet him. Hunt replied, "Have no band, and cut out the banquets; keep your money for something useful."

He loved Arizona, saying, "I have shared her vicissitudes while she has retrieved my misfortunes."

Hunt died at his Phoenix home on December 24, 1934, at the age of seventy-five. He left instructions for his burial:

It is my wish and desire to be burried [sic] on some Butte or Mountain overlooking the Salt River Valley. I came to Arizona in July 1881, this has been my home and constant endeavor since those days in trying to make Arizona a great Commonwealth. The people of this state had been good to me and in my last sleep I want to be burried [sic] that I may in my spirit overlook this splendid Valley that in the years to come will be the mecca of those that love beautiful things, and in a state where the people rule.

He is buried under an odd white pyramid atop a bluff in Phoenix's Papago Park.

Barry Goldwater

Barry Goldwater, the father of modern-day conservatism, has been called the most successful loser in American presidential history. In the early 1970s a Gallup poll showed that Goldwater was the tenth most admired man in the world, right behind Pope Paul VI.

"I guess there isn't a man alive with whom so many people disagree so often and like so much," said 60 *Minutes* commentator Andy Rooney in 1978.

He had one of the most recognizable faces of his time, with

the square jaw, the horn-rim glasses, and the knowing smile. His straight-talking, tell-it-like-it-is responses gave him the appearance of a charming curmudgeon. You always knew where Barry Goldwater stood.

Historian Doris Kearns Goodwin said, "There was a civility and a camaraderie that he had that belied some of that fastest lip in the West, which he was called sometimes, because he spoke off the cuff a little bit too much."

Charles Lichenstein, research director for his 1964 presidential campaign, said Goldwater's philosophy was simply "If I want to go to hell, I want to go to hell in my own way."

Barry Morris Goldwater was born on January 1, 1909, in Phoenix. His Jewish ancestors had come to Arizona in the late 1800s as merchants, moving to Prescott after financial difficulties in Phoenix in the 1870s. "We went broke in more damn places that you can shake a stick at," Goldwater said. "We went broke in some places you never heard of."

One day his father, Baron, said he wanted to go back to Phoenix. Goldwater's Uncle Morris replied, "No, Phoenix will never amount to anything. All they have down there is farming, and we have the mines." "Well, they argued," Goldwater said, "and finally to settle it, they played a game of casino. And my father won. And in 1894 we moved back down to Phoenix and eventually we all made a little money."

His father married Josephine Williams, the first registered nurse in the Arizona territory, in 1907. Goldwater may have gotten his "damn the consequences" attitude from his mother, who shocked Phoenix society by smoking in public, playing golf in knickers, and driving around in the family cars. Goldwater said he grew up as "a spoiled, well-off kid. . . . I was born in a log cabin," he would joke, "equipped with a golf course, a pool table, and a swimming pool." He said he learned his politics at the knee of his Uncle Morris, who was mayor of Prescott for twenty-two years. "He firmly believed that limited government was the secret of keeping freedom," Goldwater said. "All of our efforts were directed at that."

He was raised an Episcopalian. "Neither my father nor any of our family ever took any part in the Jewish community. We never felt or talked about being half Jewish since my mother took us to the Episcopal church. It was only on entering the power circles of Washington that I was reminded I was a Jew. I never got used to being singled out in that way. . . . I've simply never practiced the Jewish faith or seen myself or our family primarily of Jewish culture. In the jargon of today's sociologist, we've been assimilated. We're American."

He attended Phoenix schools, but after a rebellious freshman year in high school, he was sent to Staunton Military Academy in Virginia, where he thrived on the rigorous discipline and military atmosphere. Graduating at the top of his class, he returned to attend the University of Arizona during the 1928–29 school year and joined Sigma Chi fraternity, an affiliation he valued throughout his life.

He left school after less than a year when his father died, and went to work in the family department store. Rising through the ranks of the firm, Goldwater became general manager at the age of twenty-seven and president a year later, a position he held until he entered the Senate in 1952. He took time out during World War II to serve in the army air corps.

He flew C-47s over the Himalayan "Hump" in Southeast Asia, at one time carrying, among other things, a Buick to China for General Chiang Kai-shek's wife, plus a lot of toiletries and dresses. "I believe I was better equipped, psychologically, to be a military officer than a politician," Goldwater said. "There's no greater service to this country than the defense of its freedom." He later became a brigadier general in the air force reserves and organized the air national guard in Arizona. He retained his interest in flying and at the age of fifty twice flew jets at the speed of sound.

After the war Goldwater returned to run the family store. A genius at figuring out what customers wanted, he developed "antsypants," men's white shorts with red ants all over them. "Just as I figured, there wasn't a woman in the world who didn't know at least one man that she'd like to send a pair of antsypants. And then I sent six pairs to Harry Truman. And that got it started . . . my God, we almost went broke selling antsypants." The Goldwater stores were sold to Associated Dry Goods Corporation of New York for $2.2 million in 1962.

Goldwater tired of the business world after the war and became involved in municipal reform. In 1949 he was persuaded to run for the city council. "Don't cuss me too much. It ain't for life, and it may be fun," he told his brother, Bob, explaining his decision to run for public office. He was elected and served as a city councilman from 1949 to 1952.

He loved Arizona and took pride in its growth. "I always said that Arizona is a 114,000-square-mile piece of heaven which just fell. . . . It's home to me—where my family is, where my heart is, where I belong. Very few people my age have had the opportunity of seeing a country transformed the way I've seen Arizona. . . . Once it was wild land and desert and open spaces—and there's still plenty of that. But I've seen this land transported into productive land, with great industry and great people and great promise of a great future. Take Phoenix. I get the greatest thrill thinking that in a small way I helped it grow, that I had something to do with its growth."

When Goldwater visited Washington to urge action on the proposed Central Arizona Project, a multibillion-dollar plan to bring Colorado River water to Tucson and Phoenix, he stopped to see Arizona's junior senator, Ernest McFarland, who had been appointed Senate majority leader in 1950. Goldwater told him, "Mac, you're out of your head. You cannot carry that [President Harry] Truman. He's going to be too heavy an anvil around your neck. Someone is going to beat you," never dreaming he would be the one to do it.

In 1952 Goldwater was elected to the U.S. Senate by a margin of 6,725 votes, upsetting McFarland, who saw himself so secure in his post that he rarely campaigned. By contrast, during the ten-month Senate campaign, Goldwater gave six hundred speeches and flew 50,000 miles in his airplane.

He was a bright, charismatic politician, but it helped that he rode in on Eisenhower's coattails. "I had no business beating Ernest McFarland," Goldwater said, "and I knew that from the day I started, but old Mac just thought he had it in the bag and just didn't come home." "I could never have been elected if it hadn't been for Democrats. . . . I'd still be back selling pants." He was referring to "Pinto Democrats," named after pinto horses. They were actually Republicans who registered as Democrats so they could have a say in which Democrat would be elected in the primaries and to take advantage of Democratic patronage.

Democrats had a 6 to 1 advantage over Republicans in voter registration. Even with Republican Howard Pyle in the governor's chair, the Arizona house had only two Republicans out of ninety seats, and the Senate had one out of twenty-eight. But the mood was changing with the influx of thousands of newcomers. In the 1952 elections Republicans were elected to thirty-five seats in the state house.

Once in the U.S. Senate, Goldwater began spreading his brand of conservatism. He was not much for proposing legislation; he had the larger view of setting conservative policy. However, he was a strong supporter of the multibillion-dollar Central Arizona Project, financed primarily by the federal government. In one of those incongruities that politicians often fall into, when Goldwater ran for president, he criticized the much smaller Tennessee Valley Authority, calling it a socialist scheme.

Goldwater was reelected in 1958, again beating McFarland.

Jim Kolbe, now a congressman from Arizona, was a Goldwater page when he was sixteen years old. "That's when I got to really know this extraordinary individual. Even then, beginning his second term in the Senate, he was a different senator, saying exactly what was on his mind, never shading his words. Some senators thought this a bit odd, others loved it, but all of them—and all of us—respected him for his candor."

In 1957 he found time to build a house on Camelback Mountain, overlooking Phoenix, which he called Be-Nun-I-Kin, Navajo for "house on the hilltop." A ham radio operator and photographer, he loved gadgets, such as the electronically operated flagpole at his home that was rigged to raise the flag at the precise moment it was struck by the rays of the morning sun. He and his wife, Peggy, whom he married in 1934 and who died in 1985, raised their four children there: Joanne, Barry Jr., Michael, and Peggy. One of them, Barry Goldwater, Jr., represented California in Congress for fourteen years.

Goldwater's 1960 bestseller, *The Conscience of a Conservative,* was one of the most successful political books in American history, selling 3.5 million copies. He wrote it, he said, "to awaken the American people to a realization of how far we had moved from the old constitutional concepts toward the new welfare state. . . . My aim is not to pass laws, but to repeal them. It is not to inaugurate new programs, but to cancel old ones that do violence to the Constitution."

He opposed the Civil Rights Act of 1964, but he was no bigot. He had integrated his own department stores, as well as the Arizona Air National Guard. He opposed the act as a violation of states' rights and property rights, even though 80 percent of congressional Republicans supported it. "It's not the government's part to make men moral," he said. "Integration should be left to the states." He opposed busing and backed prayer in schools, but thought it was a dangerous breach of the separation of powers for Congress to be telling the courts what to do.

With all the attention, Goldwater reflected in 1970 that "I found myself becoming a political fulcrum of the vast and growing tide of American disenchantment with the public policies of liberalism." In the early 1960s talk about a possible presidential bid against President Kennedy began. He thought he could win. Then came the assassination.

At that point he was not too sure about his chances for the presidency, saying it would be impossible to win against the ghost of Kennedy and Lyndon Johnson, who moved up from vice president. "We knew from the beginning that we had no chance against the man who replaced Jack Kennedy after the assassination," he said. "The country was just not ready for three presidents in three years."

His wife, Peggy, didn't want him to run for the presidency, and he wasn't so sure he wanted to, either. "In my gut, there was never a burning desire to be president. I just wanted the conservatives to have a real voice in the country. . . . Someone had to rally the conservatives, take over the Republican Party, and turn the direction of the GOP around. There was no one to do it but me. We'd lose the election but win the party," he wrote in his autobiography, *With No Apologies.* He said another reason he decided to run was to "keep the Republican Party from falling into the hands of Rockefeller and the Eastern Gang, as we called them, which we did and which allowed Nixon to run [in 1968]."

In 1963, when a columnist asked him what it might feel like to wake up as president someday, Goldwater replied, "Frankly, it scares the hell out of me." He said running for president "was like trying to stand up in a hammock."

At the Republican National Convention in 1964, he pretty much demolished his chances of winning when he uttered one of the most quoted and vilified statements of the campaign: "Extremism in the defense of liberty is no vice. Moderation in the pursuit of justice is no virtue."

Johnson campaigned on the promise that he would not

enlarge the Vietnam War and that Goldwater was a "hit-the-red-button, kill-'em candidate." Goldwater's theme was "a choice, not an echo." He called Johnson "the phoniest individual that ever came around." Johnson, in turn, called Goldwater "a raving, ranting demagogue . . . who wants to tear down society."

Johnson launched a bitter, vicious attack against Goldwater. He aired an advertisement on TV that implied that if Goldwater won, there might be nuclear incineration of children. A young girl was shown counting petals from a daisy, and as she counted, a male voice, deep and ominous, counted backward from ten, getting progressively louder. When he reached zero, a nuclear explosion went off in the background, filling the air with a nuclear cloud. The background voice said Goldwater had voted against a nuclear weapons testing ban treaty. Representative John Rhodes of Mesa called the commercial "the most heinous political crime I have ever seen."

Goldwater lost forty-four states, receiving 27 million votes versus Johnson's 43 million. But he had no regrets. "I think it made people think, and that's what politics is all about. . . . We made a lot of mistakes. . . . We made other strategic and tactical errors from the shortsighted viewpoint of an election victory. I never blamed anyone. Nor did I ever believe the media were the major reason for my defeat, although in my opinion they were unfair to us at times."

His deputy press secretary, Vic Gold, said, "Goldwater told me if he was going to lose, it would be on his terms." Former Secretary of the Interior Stewart Udall, a fellow Arizonan, said Goldwater was too honest to be president. "His candor was so pronounced that it harmed his 1964 campaign—and caused some of us to conclude that he was too honest to be president."

The success of his conservative philosophy paved the way for Ronald Reagan's eight years in the White House in the 1980s.

Goldwater had criticized Johnson for running for the Senate

while at the same time running for the vice presidency in 1960. So he refused to do the same in 1964 and gave up his Senate seat. He was out of politics for four years, a period he called "four of the most satisfying years I have had as an adult."

Goldwater never again was considered as a presidential candidate. He raised funds for the Republican Party and settled into a basement office in the Goldwater's store in Scottsdale. He was earning up to $150,000 a year in speaking fees and wrote a column for the *Los Angeles Times* that was picked up by seventy newspapers across the country.

He always had a great love for Native Americans, and the Navajos gave him the name Chischilly, or "curly-haired one." A tattoo on his left hand identified him with the Smoki dancers, a Prescott organization that performs its own versions of sacred Indian dances. He owned an extensive collection of kachina dolls that is now housed in the Heard Museum in Phoenix. Whenever there was a severe blizzard in northern Arizona, he would collect food and hay and fly it to Indian families and cattle cut off by snowdrifts. "I've probably spent more time with Arizona's Indians than any other white man," he noted.

Goldwater enjoyed cracking a good joke now and then. "Sex and politics are a lot alike," he said. "You don't have to be good at them to enjoy them."

By 1967 he was itching to return to politics and announced he would seek a return to the Senate. Polls showed him ahead of the venerable Carl Hayden, who would be ninety-one years old when reelected. Hayden decided to quit while he was on top. Other candidates considering a run were Stewart Udall, Congressman Morris Udall, and Hayden aide Roy Elson. Only Elson decided to oppose Goldwater, and he lost by 69,000 votes.

Because he had resigned to run for president, Goldwater had no seniority when he was elected to replace Carl Hayden. He seemed to lose interest in the Senate, as shown by his poor record of attendance and the few bills he submitted. Historian Peter Iverson noted that Goldwater's greatest strength lay not in the details of a particular bill but in the bigger picture.

Legislation is "not his thing," said Representative Rhodes. "Barry has always painted with a broad brush, and I say that without criticism. All of us have to do what we are best at. He has never been known as a detail man."

Goldwater did support a wilderness bill for Arizona. "I want it to stay that way [wild]. The minute you create a wilderness area a lot of these Easterners have to have paved roads to get in, and they have to have hot dog stands, motels and the whole damn country is ruined." If there was any vote he would take back, he said, it was the one that created the Glen Canyon Dam, "because it was the most beautiful canyon in the whole world. It wasn't as big as the Grand Canyon, but for sheer red limestone cliffs coming down 700 and 800 feet."

He gained attention when House and Senate leaders, including Rhodes, worked to persuade Nixon to resign in 1973. Goldwater told Nixon that the Republicans in Congress were unwilling and unable to stop his impeachment and conviction should he remain in office. Nixon announced his resignation the next day.

He called Nixon "the most dishonest individual I have ever met in my life. . . . As far as I'm concerned, Nixon can go to China and stay there. . . . He lied to the people, he lied to his friends in Congress, including me. That was the last straw. . . . I was wrong in protecting him as long as I did."

Goldwater won his last term in 1980, beating Bill Schulz, a multimillionaire apartment-house developer, who based his campaign on Goldwater's absenteeism from the Senate. Indeed, he had missed about half of the votes while in the Senate from 1969 to 1974. Although this last time he won, the margin was less than 10,000, which was small for him.

During his final term Goldwater's health began to deteriorate. He had hip surgery and a triple coronary bypass operation and for a time was confined to a wheelchair. He seemed to mellow when he returned to the Senate.

Goldwater was primarily responsible for the unanimous Senate passage of the Defense Department Reorganization Act of 1986, which streamlined command channels at the Pentagon. It was "the only goddamn thing I've done in the Senate that's worth a damn," he said.

In the 1980s and '90s he defended legal abortion, voting consistently to uphold the 1973 Supreme Court ruling that legalized abortion. "They think I've turned liberal because I believe a woman has a right to an abortion. That's a decision that's up to the pregnant woman, not up to the pope or some do-gooders or the religious right. It's not a conservative issue at all," he said in his typical outspoken manner.

Later in his life he was honored by Planned Parenthood. His first wife, Peggy, had helped found the Arizona organization in 1937 and with other volunteers had founded the Mother's Health Clinic, which gave out birth control devices. She was a close personal friend of Margaret Sanger, founder of the American birth control movement.

Goldwater also backed homosexual rights. "You don't have to agree with it, but they have a constitutional right to be gay." He had a grandson who was gay and HIV-positive. About President Clinton's "don't-ask, don't-tell policy," Goldwater remarked, "You don't have to be 'straight' to fight and die for your country. You just have to shoot straight." When Representative Kolbe saw Goldwater in 1996, not long after Kolbe revealed he was gay, he admitted he had some trepidation about what his old boss would say or think. He said Goldwater took his hand in his still strong grip and said, "Good for you. Doesn't make a damn bit of difference to me."

He also criticized the religious right, saying that Jerry Falwell needed "a swift kick in the ass." Annoyed by the religious right's political activities, he said, "I get damn tired of those political preachers telling me what to believe in and do." His claim in 1989 that the Republican Party had been taken over by a "bunch of kooks" was a reference to forces supporting TV evangelist Pat Robertson.

On all of these issues, Goldwater's stand was not seen by most Republicans as a betrayal of his conservative ideas but as a culmination of "frontier libertarianism that showed a stiff opposition to government's poaching beyond the fence of privacy."

Nonetheless, he never wavered from his opposition to gun control or his belief that women should stay home to raise their children instead of working. Lee Edwards, one of his many biographers—and a former campaign aide—remarked, "He was willing to stand up, by God, for what we believed in. It took our breath away." As he got older, he just became a little more prickly and a lot more outspoken on an issue he loved—freedom. "I would challenge anybody who knew who Barry Goldwater was to establish anything that shows his basic philosophy ever really changed," said Republican Representative John Shadegg of Arizona, whose father, Stephen, ran Goldwater's campaigns.

In 1992 Goldwater stated, "I don't like being called the New Right; I'm an old, old son-of-a-bitch. I'm a conservative." That same year he married Susan Schaffer Wechsler, a health care executive. His first wife, Peggy, had died in 1985.

In a 1994 commentary published in the *Arizona Republic,* Goldwater wrote, "The positive role of limited government has always been the defense of these fundamental principles (individual rights and liberties). The conservative movement is founded on the simple tenet that people have the right to live life as they please, as long as they don't hurt anyone else."

When he died on May 29, 1998, he was in his own bed, overlooking the valley he loved and surrounded by family. "He died as he lived: with dignity, courage, and humility," a family statement said.

After his death historian Michael Beschloss remarked that Goldwater had lived long enough to hear a Democratic president, Bill Clinton, say in his State of the Union address that the era of big government was over. "That's what Barry Goldwater lived his political career to hear from a Democrat."

Rose Mofford

Former Governor Rose Mofford best exemplifies how government was one avenue to success for women in a male-dominated society in the last half of the twentieth century, though her rise to power was slow and laborious. Except for one brief period in her early years, she spent her entire career in service to Arizona, beginning with a job as a secretary and culminating in her appointment as governor after Evan Mecham's impeachment.

When she decided to retire rather than seek election to the office, she said, "This one I have to call for Rosie. I just wonder how many more years can one person serve?" She had served the people of Arizona for fifty-one years, beginning her career at age seventeen. During her years of state government service, she dealt personally with twelve of the state's sixteen governors.

Rose Perica Mofford was born on June 10, 1922, in Globe, the youngest of six children born to Austrian immigrants John and Frances Perica. She was the first female class president at Globe High School and graduated in 1939 as valedictorian and with the highest grade point average ever earned at the school. She excelled at softball and basketball and even turned down the chance to play professional basketball with the American Redheads.

Her first job, at the age of seventeen, was as secretary to Joe Hunt, the state treasurer. When he was elected to the Tax Commission, she followed and stayed there until 1945. She left for a year to become business manager of *Arizona Highways,* then returned to the Tax Commission to work thirteen more years as an executive secretary. When Hunt retired in 1960, she was fired because the new commissioner wanted a man to fill the spot.

While at the Tax Commission, in 1957 she married T. R. "Lefty" Mofford, who was deputy state treasurer and had been a founding father of the Phoenix Police Department. During their ten-year marriage they tried unsuccessfully to adopt children and opened their home to foster children. The Moffords were later divorced, but Rose kept her married name.

After leaving the Tax Commission, she went to work for the Secretary of State's office for the next fifteen years. In 1975, needing a change in career direction, Mofford became assistant director of the State Revenue Department, formerly the Tax Commission. In 1977, when Governor Raul Castro was appointed ambassador to Argentina, Secretary of State Wes Bolin, a Democrat, ascended to the governorship. Dozens of friends Mofford had acquired over her thirty-six years in public service pressured Bolin to appoint her, a lifelong Democrat, to his old job.

According to Arizona State University Professor Marianne Jennings, Mofford "brought a personal style, work ethic and level of conscientiousness to the office that included her now famous returns of telephone calls, responses to the mail, and her penchant for keeping and being on time for appointments." She even had her home telephone number listed in the phone book.

"I try never to be late," Mofford said. "I make it a point to leave in plenty of time. I don't want to get the reputation of being late. A woman has a harder row to hoe in some ways. You can't let people think you are all hot and bothered."

Mofford became a fixture in the Secretary of State's office, where she was known for years as the tall, friendly woman with a "hive of spun white hair atop her head like a crown" and a sense of humor. She spent long hours at the job she loved. "I work every day like I was running for reelection and the race was tight. That's the only way I know how. That's what my mother taught me." It worked, as she was elected in her own right in 1978 and then reelected in 1982 and 1986. She also served as president of the National Association of Secretaries of State in 1982 and 1983.

Mofford was next in the line of succession in 1978 when Bolin died in office, but state law prohibited her from moving up because she was not elected. Instead, the post went to the second in line, Attorney General Bruce Babbitt, also a Democrat.

Mofford finally got her chance in 1988.

In 1986 Glendale car dealer Evan Mecham was elected governor, and Mofford was propelled into national prominence. Almost immediately Mecham was faced with impeachment, a recall movement, and criminal charges resulting from alleged misuse of campaign funds. As secretary of state, Mofford had to verify the legitimacy of the signatures on recall petitions and, when the necessary number was reached, schedule a recall election.

Before the election could be held, however, Mecham was impeached, and Mofford became acting governor until the senate voted to remove Mecham from office. By that time she had been elected in her own right as secretary of state. In April 1988 Mofford became Arizona's eighteenth governor and first female chief executive, appointed to finish the remaining thirty months of Mecham's term.

Upon taking office, she released a statement that said:

> Members of the press and my fellow Arizonans. This is a difficult hour in our state's history. My heart goes out to the entire Mecham family. Today, we have reached the end of difficult times in Arizona. I know the decision made by the senate today was not reached lightly. It is time to put all that behind us and move forward. Today our constitution has worked. Our elected representatives have spoken. As we work together to bind the wounds of the last few months, let us purge our hearts of suspicion and hate. Today, none of us are Republicans, none of us are Democrats. We are all Arizonans. Let us go forward together as Arizonans. I ask all of you for your prayers and your support, both for me and the Mecham family. I did not ask for this burden. But I do not shrink from the job before me. With God's help, I will not let you down.

Mofford was not inexperienced at the job; technically, she had served as Arizona's chief executive during the 890 days Babbitt was out of state, primarily in 1987 and 1988, when he was seeking the Democratic nomination for president. She had also had the task of maintaining stability and order during the dark days prior to the senate's conviction and overcoming the uncertainty that existed afterward. On short notice she put together a staff that saw her through the difficult transition of power from Mecham to her.

Although she managed to return calm to the governor's office and state government, her thirty months in office were not seen as exceptional in moving the state forward. The legislature seized the power the governor's office lost in the struggle over Mecham's removal, and Mofford was seen to be no more than a caretaker.

She was criticized for treating the job as a ceremonial position. She once suggested to business and civic leaders that they drink their milk, eat cookies, take a nap every afternoon and "draw and paint and sing and dance." But she also exercised her veto power eighteen times while in office. She was criticized for commuting the sentences of two convicted murderers—a decision she later rescinded. Her admission that she had been unaware of the gruesome nature of the crimes sparked questions about her competency.

She pushed for a supercollider project in Arizona and was criticized when the state's efforts were labeled "amateurish." Much of her administration was in limbo until she presented her first budget in 1989. Its emphasis on education reflected her belief that a well-educated populace would help the economy to grow and attract future investment.

At first she said she would be a candidate for a full term, but then on January 18, 1990, she announced she would not run, despite raising $375,000 in campaign funds. She claimed that her health played no role in her decision, although she had just undergone gall bladder surgery and had several minor ailments. Rather, she said, she wanted the time to travel, play golf, and "attend my class reunion this year . . . to see if they look as old as I do," and "be able to go to a sports event and not have to leave to go somewhere else. . . . I was here when I felt the state needed me, and I [feel] that I'm leaving the state in good hands."

Rose Mofford was almost universally praised for being a calming influence on the state after Mecham's removal from office. House Minority Leader Art Hamilton, a Phoenix Democrat, said, "I think the legacy of Governor Mofford will be that at a time when the state was in desperate trouble, at a time when our reputation was being questioned around the country, at a time when we were so politically unstable, she did bring stability to government."

Bob Corbin, the state's Republican attorney general, likened Mofford's takeover of the executive office with Gerald Ford's efforts to restore stability after President Nixon resigned: "I think Rose did the same thing."

When asked how she would like to be remembered, Mofford said as "the governor who loved her state and would die for it." What did she think her legacy was? "I hope they will remember me as a caring governor because I have cared about everyone else in Arizona."

Sam Steiger

Sam Steiger is known as much for his colorful language and antics as for his political career, which reaches from U.S. representative to senatorial candidate to mayor of Prescott, Arizona. He has often been described as a love-him-or-hate-him politician.

"I'm pretty hard on people," he said. "That's because I'm lazy and I want to make the point quickly, so I call someone a scum bag."

Among his many antics were shooting to death two burros that he said attacked him ("I could invent a cure for cancer,

and they would remember me as the guy who shot the burros")
and painting a crosswalk from the Yavapai County Courthouse
in Prescott to the saloons across the street on Whiskey Row.
("Everybody says I was drunk and we did it after the bars closed.
In fact, it was still daylight when we did it. I know because I had
to get home afterward.")

His opinion of government? "We're talking about people
who can't organize a two-car funeral."

To say that Steiger is no more than a curmudgeon who tosses
out biting one-liners with reckless abandon would be to ignore
the man's complexities.

Samuel Steiger was born on March 10, 1929, in New York
City, where he attended elementary and high school. He went on
to Cornell University and Colorado A&M before becoming a
commissioned officer in the U.S. Army. He served as a tank pla-
toon leader in Korea and was awarded the Silver Star and the
Purple Heart.

He moved to Prescott after the Korean War. Today, he says,
the Prescott he loved "is beyond recovery. . . . I don't think it's
reparable. Prescott might be salvageable, if you could somehow at
least manage this insanity." The changes that came with growth
seem to bother him most. "When I came to Prescott, my future
father-in-law's phone number was seven. Now we're sort of the
Sun City of the north. Old people don't make good neighbors,"
says Steiger, who is in his seventies. "I used to tell my kids that
when we got 10 stop lights in Prescott it was time to move. It
came and went so quickly. Now we've got 150."

He also has cruel words for his adopted Arizona as it is today. "Arizona is like a lot of the Southwest," he says. "One of
the things it is, is a home for losers. People come here because
they've screwed up somewhere else. The truth is, the reason they
screwed up had nothing to do with where they were. They're just
screw-ups. Arizona, I think, has a proportionately larger share of
screw-ups."

Now divorced, he has been married twice and has three adult children: Lewis, Gail, and Delia Rebecca.

Steiger engaged in ranching and horse breeding in Prescott before he was elected to two terms in the state senate from 1960 to 1964. The *Arizona Republic* referred to him in 1964 as "independent, friendly, quick-witted, very outspoken, crazy over horses and wears an infectious smile." In 1966 he ran successfully for the U.S. House of Representatives as a Republican and was reelected to four more two-year terms.

When he went to Congress, he reportedly said that he wouldn't hire some of his colleagues to operate a wheelbarrow. While a freshman congressman, he gave a speech on the House floor in which he said it was "an irrefutable fact of life that the elected official is regarded by those who elect him as capable of the most flagrant dishonor." Such rhetoric led former Interior Secretary Stewart Udall to call Steiger "a bomb thrower" while he was in Congress.

He admitted making mistakes in Congress. "I voted for OSHA [Occupational Safety and Health Act] because I didn't want to be perceived as being against safety," he said. "That is where cowardice crept in." In 1974 he earned an award as the nation's outstanding conservative legislator.

Steiger claimed he was one of those responsible for Arizona congressman John Rhodes's ascent to minority leader in the House. "All John had was me," he said. "I played a major role by brokering his candidacy. I had the confidence of the membership."

It was while in Congress in 1975 that the burro incident came up. According to Steiger, a man from Paulden, Arizona, was letting as many as 150 burros run loose. Some residents said they were scaring children at bus stops. "People had been ragging me about the burros," he recalled.

Then one evening while he was visiting his brother-in-law, who was a highway patrolman, a call came in about burros on the road. Steiger took a gun and approached the burros to get a look at their brands. When the animals became aggressive toward him, he shot two of them. He then called the sheriff's office and admitted to the shooting. From then on, he said, he was known as "the jackass slayer." The next weekend the state livestock sanitary board rounded up the burros and shipped them to a holding facility.

In 1976 Steiger sought the Senate seat held by the retiring Paul Fannin. He entered the Republican primary against fellow congressman John Conlan, the son of major league umpire Jocko Conlan. The primary turned into one of the nastiest and most divisive in state party history. Conlan sent out letters to supporters asking whether they really wanted "a Jew from New York telling Arizona what to do." Steiger countered by claiming that "Godzilla would make a better senator than John Conlan." Steiger won, but the vicious primary fight may have hurt him in the general election, when Democrat Dennis DeConcini, the Pima County attorney, beat him decisively. "Conlan was a right-wing lunatic," Steiger said, "and I was a right-wing philosopher."

In 1978 he was defeated in a bid to return to the state senate. In the meantime he meddled in Prescott politics, trying to shape public policy to his liking. People loved him or hated him, calling him either "dear old Sam" or "that son of a bitch." Ken Bennett, a councilman in the 1980s, said Prescott liked Steiger when he was a "brash young congressman out in Washington telling people what to do. But they liked him less when he came back here and started telling our people what to do. Sam was the kiss of death in Prescott for a while. His popularity was at an all-time low. But he was back to being a hero with that crosswalk."

Steiger tells the crosswalk story this way.

In 1986 he opposed a decision by the city eliminating a crosswalk in the middle of the street from the courthouse to Whiskey Row, a string of saloons. He decided to take action. "That was not out of character for me," he said. "The city had decided that since we were self-insured they couldn't afford the crosswalk. It had never been a problem and I just decided, what the heck, let's put it back."

He denies the persistent legend that he painted it with a brush at night after an evening of drinking on Whiskey Row. In reality, he used a parking-lot striping machine. He was arrested. "They took me in. There's a great picture of five cops and me with my hands on the car." He defended himself in the trial, and so many people wanted to see the trial it had to be moved to the federal courthouse. "My argument was it wasn't criminal damage," he says. "It was historical preservation." He was found not guilty. "I don't think the jury ever left the box. They voted right there."

Ken Bennett summed up the story by saying, "[the Arizona Department of Transportation] wouldn't paint it, the city and county won't stand up to the state to get it done, but Sam Steiger is willing to have a few beers and then go out and do it himself. People loved it."

If politics makes strange bedfellows, as the cliché goes, that would never be so true as when Steiger became special assistant to Governor Evan Mecham in 1986, during his short term before impeachment. Steiger stirred up controversy, and while it didn't measure up to Mecham's, it caused a furor nonetheless.

While special assistant, he was convicted of "theft by extortion" for threatening a parole board member with his job if he didn't vote the way the governor wanted. The state parole board was one of thirteen agencies Steiger oversaw in his job. The case was later thrown out when an appeals court declared that such hardball politics was not extortion. "It was printed in the paper that I had abused this poor guy," Steiger said, "but all I did was explain to him how things worked. He was our appointee and I was an enforcer—that was my role. My job was to see that the governor's will was carried out.

"I thought I was going to jail, which probably wouldn't have worked out so well. I don't think I'd do very well in jail." The court received more than 140 letters in support of Steiger, including some from old political acquaintances. Morris Udall, a former House colleague, asked leniency for "an old antagonist and friend whose quick tongue and cold political instincts have gotten him into trouble several times."

He was sentenced to three years' probation and a fine, but the sentence was short-lived. Three months later the Arizona Court of Appeals overturned the decision and recommended the legislature look into refining an extortion statute the court called "vaguely drafted." Steiger said he spent $140,000 defending himself. "I was a long time digging out of that hole."

That and other experiences with lawyers led him to write the humorous book *Kill the Lawyers!* in 1990.

Steiger took two shots at the governor's job. He ran in 1982 as a Libertarian and received 36,526 votes, or 5 percent of the total, and in 1990 as a Republican, in a race he called "old Sam's last roundup." He was the only candidate to admit he wanted to be governor to satisfy his own ego. "I'm running for governor, warts and all, not only because I can make a real difference in this state, but because it will make me feel good," he said.

Others in the race included Democrat Terry Goddard and Republicans Fife Symington and Evan Mecham. One Republican official said only Symington and Steiger had a chance to beat Goddard—"Fife because he's got all that money and Steiger because he's so damn likable. You can always get money, but you can't buy that kind of charm. Steiger is a bigger threat." But Symington won the primary hands down, then went on to win the governorship in a runoff election.

Steiger was not quite through with politics yet. Back in Prescott he continued to decry the environmental degradation of his beloved hometown, mainly via a television show on KUSK, which reaches as far as Yuma and Flagstaff. He read snippets from newspapers and magazines on the air in a somewhat crusty, crabby tone.

"I don't really have a message. I just tell people what I think about different issues. A lot of people hate me, but I think there's a perception of candor there. I get letters all the time that say, 'I don't agree with you, but I like the way you tell it.'" *Arizona Republic* reporter Dave Walker called Steiger's show "anti-television, the kind of clock-stopping programming that caused bored Rooskies to overthrow communism in favor of Melrose Place and MTV."

Tonya Mock, who produced the program, said: "People ask me what it's like to produce Sam's show. I say, 'I don't produce Sam's show. I tell him to comb his hair, put on his microphone and tell him how many calls he has. How can you produce Sam Steiger?'"

Steiger returned to elected office in 1999 when he decided to seek the mayor's job, running on a slow-the-growth campaign. "People kept saying, 'stop bitching and do something about [growth]' so I did," he said. The city's new ban on water-gun use during the city's annual Fourth of July celebration was a campaign issue. Steiger scoffed at the "tradition." "That's not a tradition," he said. "The tradition on the Fourth of July was to get drunk and fall down in the streets." With his name recognition, personality, and slow-growth stance, he was able to beat two-term incumbent Paul Daly by winning more than half the votes in a four-way race.

After he was elected mayor, a reporter asked him how it felt to be back in public office. "It sucks," he said. Same old Sam.

Bruce Babbitt

He is the perfect combination of eastern slick and western hick, as comfortable in blue pin-stripe suits and button-down white shirts as he is in checked flannel shirts and high-top boots. Bruce Babbitt is at home as much in the conference room as on the Colorado River, rafting through the Grand Canyon.

    He is tall and rangy, almost scarecrow-like, and his craggy face is that of a native of the West, but his intellect was honed in the ivy halls of Notre Dame and Harvard. His speech is precise, eloquent, and seldom hackneyed. Although cerebral, shy, and policy-oriented, he has exhibited great skill in working with people to achieve his goals when compromise has been difficult.

His views were shaped as a boy in the high mountain plateaus of northern Arizona, refined as a student in eastern schools, and sharpened as a witness to southern poverty. His experiences led him to great ambitions that may have fallen short, yet he served his country well for almost forty years.

Babbitt came from pioneer Arizona stock. His family arrived in Flagstaff four years after the railroad, traveling across country from Cincinnati, Ohio. The Babbitts became wealthy trading with Indians and ranchers through the Babbitt Brothers Trading Company. From modest beginnings trading for Navajo rugs and cattle, the family business developed into a vast ranching and retailing empire spread across northern Arizona.

Bruce Edward Babbitt, the son of Paul James and Frances Babbitt, was born on June 27, 1938, in Los Angeles but reared in Flagstaff. His parents believed in discipline and participation in activities outside the schoolhouse. His mother attempted to develop his cultural skills, and his father, an amateur anthropologist, stressed the outdoors, particularly rock and ruin hunting. Bruce developed an interest in geology that he would cultivate in college.

He enjoyed the outdoors as a youth, spending his time hiking and climbing. Even today he shuns sports like golf and tennis, choosing instead to hike or fish. He has remained in top physical condition. While governor, he beat well-trained Department of Public Safety agents hiking out of the Grand Canyon by one or two hours.

Babbitt had little interest in the family business and left home in 1958 to attend Notre Dame University, graduating magna cum laude with a bachelor's degree in geology. His first political success came when he was elected student body president. After graduation he won a Marshall scholarship and attended the University of Newcastle in England, where he received a master of science degree for a thesis on the volcanic geology of northern Arizona.

While at Newcastle, he spent the summer of 1961 with a crew from the Gulf Oil Corporation that was looking for oil in Bolivia. What struck him most during his stay in South America was the abject poverty he witnessed, an experience that helped convince him to leave geophysics and seek a life that encompassed social action.

After his return to the United States, he enrolled in Harvard Law School, graduating in 1965. That year he joined the civil rights march in Selma, Alabama, where again he took notice of poverty. After he was admitted to the Arizona Bar, he worked as a special assistant to the director of VISTA until 1967. A VISTA official described Babbitt as "very practical, realistic and a believer. There are believers who perhaps may be naive and others who are realistic. He was a believer who was realistic."

At VISTA he learned about waste and inefficiency in the government and developed a distaste for huge federal programs as the means to correcting social wrongs. "The war on poverty bore some good fruit," he said, "but what I learned was you can't force thoroughgoing social change from the top down. The whole war on poverty had a certain kind of arrogance. . . . It could not be a lasting process of change when it depended upon GS-7s hired in Washington dispensing federal money with terms and conditions that they prescribed in local communities."

He returned to Arizona to practice law in Phoenix and married Hattie Coons in 1969. They would have two children, Christopher and T.J. One day in 1972, while representing the Navajo nation in U.S. District Court over legislative boundaries on the reservation, he decided to run for attorney general. "A light sort of went on," he said, "and I thought, 'My God, the attorney general has the largest law firm in the state devoted to the defense of racial discrimination, and what it really ought to be is a public-interest law firm."

At the time he was also counsel for the Arizona Wildlife Federation, the Maricopa Legal Aid Society, and the Arizona Newspapers Association, three organizations that gave him great exposure throughout the state. He believed his old Arizona name and his background in government would serve him well with voters. But the intellectual and shy Babbitt was uncomfortable with the role of candidate. His wife, Hattie, described him as "a tall, skinny, intellectual ectomorph without any public-speaking ability."

Nevertheless, he was elected attorney general in November 1974 and immediately began attacking land fraud cases. In a highly publicized case, he prosecuted the murderer of *Arizona Republic* investigative reporter Don Bolles. Success led him to eye higher office, and he gave some thought to running against Barry Goldwater for senator or running for governor. But before he was forced to make a decision, Governor Wesley Bolin died on March 4, 1978. As the next in line of succession, Babbitt became Arizona's sixteenth—and youngest, at thirty-nine—governor.

In the fall he ran for a full term against Glendale car dealer Evan Mecham and was elected by a 52 to 48 percent margin. He won again four years later, beating senate president Leo Corbet with 62 percent of the vote.

Despite his intellectual and somewhat aloof manner, Babbitt was able to pull the legislature together to get legislation passed. One supporter said of him, "[He] is not an inclusive man. . . . People feel excluded on frequent occasion." He may have been conciliatory, but he still vetoed twenty-one bills in 1979 and thirty more over the next two years, more than any previous governor. He also had to cope with the influx of almost 600,000 newcomers to Arizona, which put a heavy demand on governmental services. He proved to be the model of a centrist Democrat. One of his most important acts was gaining passage in 1986 of a water quality act that the *Los Angeles Times* described as "perhaps the nation's toughest law to protect underground water." To win approval, he had to bring together farmers, environmentalists, industry, rural and urban interests, and utilities—no easy task.

Despite a grueling schedule, he authored two books, *Color and Light: The Southwest Canvasses of Louis Akin* in 1973 and *Grand Canyon: An Anthology* in 1978.

Babbitt served as chairman of the Democratic Governors Association in 1985. Not long after assuming that office, he told the Democratic National Committee, "This party has to set a new course. . . . We must reject a lazy orthodoxy which tends to view the future as a linear project of the past." He urged Democrats to reconcile their progressive tradition with fiscal reality and was one of the first major Democrats to endorse Reagan's tax simplification plan. Calling the Democrats "a party of the past and the party of the status quo," he urged them to "crawl out of this cathedral of orthodoxy. My instincts tell me the time is at hand."

A key to Babbitt's success as a Democratic governor in conservative Arizona was his recognition of the strengths of Reagan/Goldwater politics and his ability to adapt to overcome the Democrats' inability to deal with them. He saw that if the Democrats were going to wrench the White House away from the Republicans, they would have to change their tactics. He wanted to be the one to advance that cause.

In 1986, as he was preparing to leave office, Babbitt declared a paid holiday to honor the birthday of the late Martin Luther King, Jr., despite the legislature's refusal to go along with him and the attorney general's ruling that the action was unconstitutional. His critics said Babbitt wanted to use the proclamation to gain favor with black voters across the nation because of his presidential ambitions.

Indeed, he began exploring a run for the presidency after he left the governor's office in 1987. His would be "the darkest of dark horse" bids, he said. The *New York Times* said Babbitt had "emerged as one of the most conspicuous spokesmen and practitioners of neoliberalism, a philosophy that generally blends traditional Democratic goals on civil rights and social justice with fiscal restraint and limits on the size of government and the influence of special interest groups." He also considered running for the Senate seat of retiring Barry Goldwater. But the possibility of running against a brash former Vietnam prisoner of war, John McCain, and the attention being accorded him as a presidential candidate caused him to reconsider. Babbitt was hoping that neoliberalism would change Democratic politics in much the same way Goldwater changed Republican politics. In fact, it was the kind of politics that Bill Clinton embraced in 1992.

"In the West, at least in the Mountain West," Babbitt said, "liberals believe government should have a strong role in civil rights, education, health, populism, but it's combined with a certain kind of independence and skepticism of government, and a readiness to question whether government programs are necessary. Liberals must learn that cutting budgets and imposing restraints is just as important as the development of new programs."

He failed to generate much enthusiasm for his presidential bid, tallying less than double digits in public opinion polls. His campaign ended when he finished sixth in a field of seven in New Hampshire, the first primary election in a campaign eventually won by Massachusetts Governor Michael Dukakis. George H. W. Bush beat Dukakis for the White House.

In 1987 Babbitt became a partner in the law firm of Steptoe and Johnson in Washington, D.C., where his practice focused on environmental issues. He also served as national president of the League of Conservation Voters. He was probably best remembered during his tenure as league president for remarking, "We must identify our enemies and drive them into oblivion."

In 1992 President-elect Bill Clinton nominated Babbitt to be secretary of the interior, a position that generally goes to a westerner. He would be the second Arizonan to serve in the post;

the first was Stewart Udall, who ran the Department of Interior during the eight years of the Kennedy and Johnson administrations. Babbitt's nomination to head the 75,000-employee department was met with near-universal acclaim.

As interior secretary, he would oversee 500 million acres of national parks, monuments, wilderness areas, wildlife refuges, forests, rangelands, and recreation areas. Supporters said he would be adept at reconciling competing demands because of his experience as governor. Udall said about Babbitt, "Intellectually, he is well prepared. My advice to him is to stay eight years, and if he does, he can be one of the best interior secretaries of this century."

A Democratic congressional aide said that to redirect the sprawling Department of Interior after twelve years of Republican rule would take a secretary with "the heart and soul of an accountant, the resolve of a marine and the thick skin of a rhinoceros." But even environmentalists wondered if Babbitt was tough enough to reorient a department that they said was a captive of commodity interests, namely, the oil, gas, and mining industries.

As interior secretary, Babbitt said he was guided by the "standard of sustainability" that constantly asks, "How will this decision affect the beauty, integrity, and availability of [the given] resources for our children?" As secretary, he also advanced the cause of self-governance for Native American tribes.

One of his first acts was to attempt to raise grazing and mining fees on public lands. Already economically distressed, the ranching and mining industries reacted with enormous hostility. Babbitt said the White House then unilaterally dropped the proposed fee increase, which infuriated the environmentalists. So within two years the Department of Interior had angered both environmentalists and development interests. Babbitt called it one of the low points of his eight years in office.

But he retained his enormous popularity with environmentalists. Early in his tenure Babbitt was mentioned as a possible

Supreme Court nominee, head of the World Bank, or ambassador to the Court of St. James's. He may have lost out as a Supreme Court nominee because environmentalists let it be known they wanted him to stay as interior secretary. They convinced Clinton that Babbitt was "indispensable and irreplaceable."

Like other Arizona politicians—Goldwater and the Udall brothers—Babbitt also had problems with the Glen Canyon Dam. While the others fretted over the loss of the canyon behind the dam, Babbitt had a different concern: its impact on the Colorado River below the dam. "Today," he told the Ecological Society of America in a 1998 speech, "you see an ice cold, Jell-O-green river, manipulated up and down, rising and falling on a daily cycle, flushed with the regularity, and predictability, of a giant toilet."

He noted that 75,000 dams had been built across the United States, blocking 600,000 miles of free-flowing rivers. About the Bureau of Reclamation, which pushed for dams and water projects across the United States, he said, "Its practices have been the most environmentally destructive of all the public land agencies. It seems to know the subsidized price of everything and the long-term value of nothing."

In the middle of his eight-year term, Babbitt was caught in a crossfire between industry and environmentalists. Environmental groups said his tendency to compromise thwarted progress on reversing the Republican agenda of the previous twelve years. The Sierra Club called him a political pawn and said that environmentalists felt betrayed. On the other side, ranchers, loggers, and western governors worried that Babbitt's conservation efforts might hurt economic considerations.

Babbitt commented this way: "It's the nature of things that interest groups of any kind won't be in 100 percent agreement with people who have responsibility for administering and executing the laws. My job isn't to placate the opponents. My job is to listen and to learn and to put together something that is reasonable in the context of these large complicated systems. My real audience is the 80 percent who are not on either side. That's the bottom line, and that's who I'm really speaking to."

He was even berated in his home state, where he was treated as a prodigal son. State lawmakers criticized him for turning his back on the cattle and lumber industries, which had helped create the Babbitt empire in Arizona. Republican Governor Fife Symington stated, "I think he's made some decisions which really have had an adverse impact on our state. I'm certain that he's created difficulties for himself here but that may be of little consequence to him now at this point in his life."

Babbitt responded, "I don't take personal offense to anything. . . . I've been in this game a long time. You can try to get a response out of me, and you're just not going to get it out of me. This is a job for grownups."

Babbitt remained eight years in office, but the jury is still out on whether he was one of the best interior secretaries. His legacy is mixed at best, perhaps laden down by an Indian gaming rights controversy that resulted in a nineteen-month investigation by an independent counsel appointed by Attorney General Janet Reno. Because a dog track in Hudson, Wisconsin, was losing money, the track's owner and three Chippewa tribes decided to change it into a gambling casino in 1993. The change was approved by the Department of Interior's Bureau of Indian Affairs. Other Indian tribes with casinos objected and hired lobbyist Patrick O'Connor, a former treasurer of the Democratic National Committee, to fight for their interests. O'Connor lobbied President Clinton and top officials of the Democratic National Committee. On July 14, 1995, the Interior Department reversed the approval. A year later O'Connor's clients donated $370,000 to the Democratic Party and the Clinton campaign. The special prosecutor was appointed to look into whether the campaign contribution had influenced the Interior Department's—hence, Babbitt's—decision.

The independent counsel interviewed 450 witnesses and examined more than 630,000 pages of documents at a cost of $4 million. No charges were ever brought. A relieved Babbitt called the investigation "a permanent culture of the criminalization of political differences." He said that "if you are going to be in a high-profile position, the first thing you'd better do is have some lawyer's insurance. . . . The worse moments were when I got hauled up before a Senate investigating committee, then a House investigating committee, then the Justice Department, then the FBI, then a special prosecutor. And there's kind of a lynch-mob mentality in the press, to be frank. There wasn't any kind of presumption of innocence; it was a presumption of guilt. But the system ultimately does work. The justice system does work. But it wasn't pleasant."

Nonetheless, the matter tainted Babbitt's tenure in office.

In his last two years in office, Babbitt began to take steps to enhance the Clinton administration's environmental legacy. He recommended that President Clinton set aside millions of acres for national monuments, including five monuments in Arizona: the 129,000-acre Ironwood Forest National Monument north of Tucson; the 293,000-acre Vermillion Cliffs National Monument in northern Arizona; the 1 million-acre Grand Canyon–Parashant National Monument; the 72,500-acre Agua Fria National Monument near Phoenix; and the 486,000-acre Sonoran Desert National Monument. They were five of sixteen national monuments that were created and two that were expanded by the Clinton administration.

As he left office, Babbitt said that establishment of the monuments was the high point of his eight years in office. Since 2001, he has worked as an environmental lawyer in Washington, D.C.

Henry Fountain Ashurst

No more colorful politician has blessed Arizona than Henry Ashurst, one of the state's first two senators. Among his sobriquets were "Five-Syllable Henry," the "Silver-Tongued Sunbeam of the Painted Desert," and the "Dean of Inconsistency." As if those were not enough, he was even called a "many-faceted diamond among the jewels of eloquence."

He was full of bombast, polysyllabic splendor, and hot air, to be sure, but Ashurst effectively represented the Grand Canyon state for twenty-eight years. He put Arizona's interests first in the Senate, and voters returned him to office four times.

"I am not in Washington as a statesman," he said in a 1934 speech to a men's club in Arizona. "I am there as a very well-paid messenger boy doing your errands. My chief occupation is going around with a forked stick picking up little fragments of patronage for my constituents."

That same year he pointed out that Arizona had received thirty-six times as much in federal grants as it had paid in taxes. "Statesmanship," he said, "does not consist solely of taking dollars out of Uncle Sam's pockets, but I cite these statistics in proof of the fact that I have not been remiss in this duty."

The *Arizona Daily Star* wrote on June 18, 1935: "Many a person in Arizona has gone to hear Henry Ashurst make a speech prepared to scoff at his flowery oratory and has remained to vote for him, not because what he said was profound or because his policies appealed to them but because after hearing him they couldn't help liking the cuss."

From cowboy to lumberjack, from sheriff's deputy to stenographer, from newspaperman to justice of the peace, from lawyer to politician, Ashurst made a name for himself across the nation as one of the great "spread eagle" orators of the twentieth century.

He earned the title of "Dean of Inconsistency" because he changed viewpoints so often, sometimes right in the middle of a debate. "There never has been superadded to these vices of mine the withering, embalming vice of consistency," he said.

Once, while advocating prohibition, he voted for 3.2 percent beer. When questioned about his reversal, he remarked, "There's nothing strange about my shift," he said. "I went to bed as a dry one night, and woke up to find that I was all wet." Another time he cast four votes on bills that would give World War I veterans bonuses, two for and two against. Asked to explain, he replied, "What of it? At least I was fifty percent right, which is a pretty good record for a politician." On another occasion a friend complimented Ashurst for his reversal of views. "Thank God, Henry, you have seen the light." Ashurst replied, "No, I have merely felt the heat."

Ashurst was bothered little by the criticism of inconsistency. In a February 25, 1937, speech, he remarked, "Whoever in his public service is handcuffed and shackled by the vice of consistency will be a man not free to act as various questions come before him from time to time; he will be a statesman locked in a prison house, keys to which are in the keeping of days and events that are dead. Let me quote Emerson: 'A foolish consistency is the hobgoblin of little minds, adored by little statesmen.'"

He loved to speak. In his career he gave from 4,400 to 5,000 speeches. His speeches normally ran twenty to thirty minutes, but he talked for eighteen hours once in a filibuster on the Senate floor in opposition to the proposed Hoover Dam. "I suffer from cacoethes loquendi, a mania or itch for talking, and from vanity . . . and morbidity, and, as is obvious to everyone who knows me, an inborn, an inveterate flair for histrionics. . . . I am a pachydermatous. . . . I am a veritable peripatetic bifurcated volcano on behalf of Democratic principles."

He carefully researched and wrote his speeches, then tossed them aside to speak extemporaneously, relying on his razor-sharp memory to carry him through. He once claimed he could remember the entire life of St. Paul. A colleague challenged his knowledge of Aaron Burr, whereupon Ashurst spoke for two hours on Burr's life from birth to vice presidency, often citing dates and places.

U.S. Senator Barry Goldwater so loved Ashurst's speeches that he compiled fourteen of them in a book, *Speeches of Henry Fountain Ashurst of Arizona*. When Ashurst heard about it, he remarked, "But, Barry, I made over 5,000 of them."

He dressed immaculately in a black frock coat with a red carnation, striped pants, winged collar, and black-and-white cravat that adorned his large chest and stomach. Not long after he was elected to the Senate, the *Douglas International* (Douglas, Arizona) reported, "It was Mr. Ashurst's hair that caused him to be classed as a dude. He has much hair. It is rather long in back. . . . It falls down about his ears, giving him a sort of Daniel Webster halo. But it is parted exactly in the middle and 'licked' down on each side. His head looks like a country boy 'fixed up' for Sunday School."

At a meeting with King George and Queen Elizabeth in June 1939, Ashurst remarked about his attire: "I liked the Prince Albert [coat] best because the secret of keeping one's temper is to go to a function wearing tails with enough material to wrap up a sick horse. In the case of the Prince Albert, it covers with equal impartiality both the stomach and the stern, while the cutaway covers only the stern. Of course the stomach probably won't make much difference at this affair anyway."

Henry Fountain Ashurst came into this world on September 13, 1874, in a covered wagon in a lonely desert camp near the town of Winnemucca, Nevada. Of French and English ancestry, he was the second of ten children of William and Sarah Ashurst. When he was two, the family moved to a ranch at Bill Williams Mountain near Williams, Arizona. Henry was educated in Flagstaff schools.

When he was ten, he laboriously printed these words on the first page of his blue-back speller: "Henry Fountain Ashurst, United States Senator." That book rested in his library for many years.

He first became interested in public speaking when he was about fourteen, never losing sight of his goal to become a senator. He would walk miles to hear political speeches in and around Flagstaff. Ashurst later recalled that he paid little attention to the words that were spoken, choosing instead to focus on the form, manner, and language of the speeches. Asked why he liked public speaking, he replied, "I simply love speaking—just as one may like maple syrup, Beethoven, Verdi, or Longfellow, Kipling, or Shakespeare—one hardly knows why." He took some speaking lessons but learned mostly by trial and error. He learned to enunciate vowels in a baritone voice at a time when there were no microphones. And when mikes were invented he opposed them because they "transformed many men of sloppy, snippy, slovenly speech into superb speakers."

When he was seventeen or eighteen, Henry was expelled from preparatory school and sent by his father to work with a surveying crew. While working in Flagstaff, he saw a large crowd gathered around the courthouse, where he heard "a booming, vibrant" voice coming from the courtroom. The crowd was listening to the prosecutor in a murder case.

"Even then I was interested in oratory, so I decided to listen and finally wormed my way up into a crowded window . . . and there addressing the jury was a great, broad-shouldered, fine-looking man . . . holding forth with a powerful magnetic oratory. . . . I might say that right there my surveying crew lost an employee, because I stayed and listened."

Ashurst developed a love of reading in his formative years. One of his most notable characteristics when he spoke was to make literary and historical allusions gleaned from his years of reading the Bible, Shakespeare, Milton, Byron, and Longfellow. As a cowboy he carried in his saddlebags volumes by Lord Macaulay and Daniel Webster. He would deliver speeches from a stump to ranch hands who gathered around the evening campfire.

At the age of twenty, he worked as a turnkey in the county jail, where he was in charge of up to forty prisoners. He left that job to become a lumberyard worker while he studied law at night. In the ensuing two years, he was a reporter, stenographer, and justice of the peace. At age twenty-three, he was elected to the territorial house of representatives, thus beginning a forty-four-year career in politics. During his term he sponsored legislation that created what is now Northern Arizona University in Flagstaff.

Ashurst graduated from the University of Michigan Law School at the age of twenty-nine, in 1903, and a year later married a widow, Elizabeth McEvoy Renoe, who would be his constant companion until her death in 1939. He returned to Flagstaff with his bride and was elected district attorney of Coconino County.

Perhaps the best example of his oratorical hyperbole came in an opening statement in 1908 before Justice of the Peace Waltron in Winslow:

> Your honor, as I approached the trial of this case today, my heart was burdened with crushing and gloomy foreboding, the immense responsibility of my client's welfare bowed me down with apprehensions.
>
> A cold fear gripped my heart as I dwelt upon the possibility that through some oversight or shortcoming of mine there might ensue dreadful consequences to my clients, and I shrank within myself as the ordeal became imminent, yet the nearer my uncertain steps brought me to this tribunal of justice, distinguished, as it has been for years, as the one court of the rugged west where fame attended the wisdom and justice of the decisions of your honor, a serene confidence came to my troubled emotions, and the raging waters of tumultuous floods.
>
> This case, aye, I reflected that through the long years of your administration as a judge there had grown up here a halo as it were of honor and glory illuminating your honor's record, eloquent of a fame as deserved as that of the chastity of Caesar's wife, a fame that will augment with the light of years and with increasing luster, lighting the pathway of humanity down the ages so long as the heaving billows of

the stormy Mediterranean shall beat vainly upon the bleed-
ing cliffs of Gibraltar.

To which Judge Waltron replied, "Sit down, Mr. Ashurst. You
can't blow any smoke up this court's ass."

When Arizona was admitted to the Union in 1912, Ashurst
and Marcus Aurelius Smith, a Tombstone lawyer, were elected to
the U.S. Senate as Democrats. At the age of thirty-seven, he was
barely old enough to meet the age requirements of the office.

In his first speech in the Senate, Ashurst said, "Mr. President, this great new baby state is magnificent, this great new
baby state is destined to join the pantheon of other splendid states
in our fair union, this great new baby state is poised to become a
veritable paradise. We only need two things: water and lots of
good people." To which an old New England senator responded,
"If the gentleman from Arizona will forgive me, that's all they
need in Hell."

His tenure in office would bridge World War I and the Great
Depression. He served in the Arizona delegation for twenty-eight
years with the venerable Carl Hayden, who was elected first as a
representative and then as a senator. Ashurst once said, "Arizona
was fortunate to have a show horse and a work horse." It was clear
to Arizonans to whom he was referring.

Ashurst's love for northern Arizona was evident in a radio
address he made in Tucson on February 5, 1939:

Sublime as are the glories of art and architecture, Arizona
contains natural wonders of scenic grandeur sculptured
when the world was young by the Hand that sustains all
creations. For example, her petrified forests, which lived its
green millenniums and put on immortality millions of years
ago. No prose poet has ever dipped pen deep enough into
the ink of temerity to attempt a complete description of the

Grand Canyon with its mosques and minarets, its temples, pyramids, sheer cliffs, and forbidding ramparts and its colors that elude the artist's brush. . . . The fertility of Arizona's soil, the salubrity of her climate, the vastness of her mineral wealth make the lamp of Aladdin and the purse of Fortuatus appear tame and commonplace by comparison.

Despite his love for the Grand Canyon, he opposed making it a national park until national sentiment made the park inevitable. He was more interested in protecting the mining, lumber, and agricultural interests that supported him at election time. Once he saw that opposition to the park was futile, he worked for it to be created in such a manner that Arizonans could live with it. He and Hayden put together a bill that protected those interests, with boundaries drawn only to preserve geological formations and the most scenic vista points. With Arizona's opposition gone, the Grand Canyon became the nation's seventeenth park in February 1919.

Public speaking was Ashurst's consuming passion and he also liked to travel, but other than that, he had few interests. Hunting, fishing, golf, dancing, and card games, except poker, bored him. About poker he said in a 1951 speech in Virginia, "Just so long as human beings coquet the fickle jade of chance— just so long will the fascination of the true poker game allure and entertain. . . . Poker teaches self-reliance, self-control, self-respect, self-denial, and independence. But where cards are wild or are given a fictitious authority, the noble game is robbed of its romance, grace and stimulation and degenerates into a gambling scheme."

Ashurst's speaking ability captivated his Senate colleagues. They listened to him with rapt attention, they were impressed with his delivery, they enjoyed his wit and humor, they respected his long years of Senate service, and they held him in great affection and esteem. His most notable speeches were in support of the resolution to declare war on Germany in 1917, a tariff on foreign copper in 1932, the chastising of Louisiana's Huey P. Long in 1935, and the nomination of Hugo L. Black as Supreme Court justice in 1937.

His wife was less enamored of his use of long words and classical allusions. She thought he spoke too often and that any speech over twenty minutes was too long. She urged him to cut down on his many gestures, tame his shrill voice, and use shorter, easier-to-understand words. Sometimes he listened to her, but most times he went his own way.

Ashurst was asked in 1929 whether after writing a speech he went through it to remove ordinary words and insert longer ones. "And why not?" he replied. "As someone has said so brilliantly, perhaps myself, how stupid to pick coppers from the top when there are gold pieces at the bottom. I love auriferous words, and nothing delights me more than to pluck gems from the dictionary." He gave up smoking because it was "a deadly enemy to voice," and he never drank liquor when he spoke because it "will take the edge off discretion and lets down the gates of caution and prudence."

Sometimes his elocution worked against him. He tended to explain his position more than necessary. In 1914 he spoke for three hours in favor of a bill on women's suffrage, right past the time scheduled for a vote, killing a chance for the measure to pass.

Ashurst agreed to sponsor a bill in 1937 for President Franklin D. Roosevelt to increase the Supreme Court from nine members to fifteen. Roosevelt was unhappy with the Court for ruling that so many of his New Deal programs were unconstitutional. When the bill got to the Senate floor, it created a national uproar. Ashurst took so much heat that he turned around and led a fight to defeat his own bill. Afterward he received a letter from a woman in Phoenix that said, "Thank God for your courageous stand on that Supreme Court bill." Ashurst wired back to her, "Which one?"

After Ashurst's wife died in 1939, he was never the same. His heart was not into running for reelection that year. In addition, he rarely campaigned because the United States was on the brink of war, and he felt his presence as chairman of the Judiciary Committee was necessary in the nation's capital, a four-day train trip from Arizona. His opponent was Ernest McFarland, a superior court judge in Florence. McFarland did not criticize Ashurst but asked voters a simple question: "How long has it been since you've seen your senior U.S. senator?" It worked and McFarland was elected.

After his defeat Ashurst took to the Senate floor, not to wallow in pity over his loss but to reflect on the greatness of America:

> I shall not waste any time on such miserable twaddle as to say that I ought to have been elected. A man only moderately versed in statesmanship, and with only a small degree of sportsmanship, is bound to admit that in a free republic, in a government such as ours, it is the undoubted right to the people to change their servants, and to remove one and displace him with another at any time they choose, for a good reason, for a bad reason, or for no reason at all. If we are to remain a free people, it is the duty of public servants not grumpily and sourly to accept the verdict of the majority, but joyously to accept that verdict; and I joyously accept the verdict of my party. But it would by hypocrisy and pretense for me to say that I do not regret leaving the Senate. Senators, I deeply regret that I shall not be here with you when you convene in January.

Upon his defeat Turner Catledge of the *New York Times* wrote, "Sheer eloquence is best personified in the present senate by Ashurst of Arizona—the debonair, balm-tongued chairman of the Senate Judiciary Committee. Without losing one whit of his eloquence or misquoting a classical phrase, Ashurst can run the range from buffoonery to some of the most challenging remarks heard in Congress." The *Saturday Evening Post* once called Ashurst's career the "longest theatrical engagement on record."

As he closed his Senate career, he remarked that "those who seek fame do not know what it is. Those who know what it is won't seek it."

He remained in Washington, where he served on the Board of Immigration Appeals in the Department of Justice for almost two years. During that time and his subsequent retirement, he was widely sought as an after-dinner speaker.

He died on May 31, 1962, in Washington, D.C., and is buried in Prescott next to his wife.

William H. Rehnquist

Although he spent only sixteen years in Arizona, William Rehnquist, the chief justice of the United States, gained his early legal experience in the Grand Canyon state. From 1953 to 1969 he was deeply involved in Republican politics in Arizona, an association that brought him relationships that led directly to his appointment to the nation's highest court.

Even back then, controversy stalked Rehnquist, as it has during his time on the Supreme Court. He was accused on several occasions in his early political career of being a segregationist and with interfering with minority voting rights in Arizona in the 1960s. Controversy continued to dog him on the Supreme Court, right up to the court's decision on the 2000 election that enabled George W. Bush to move into the White House.

William Hubbs Rehnquist was born in Milwaukee, Wisconsin, on October 1, 1924, a first-generation American of Swedish parentage. His childhood in an upper-middle-class suburban home was relatively undistinguished. He was the son of a paper salesman who idolized popular Republican leaders such as Alf Landon, Wendell Willkie, and Herbert Hoover. His mother, a graduate of the University of Wisconsin, spoke five foreign languages and worked as a translator for several Milwaukee companies. When Rehnquist was in elementary school during the Democratic administration of Franklin D. Roosevelt, his teacher asked him about his career plans, and he replied, "I'm going to change the government."

At Sherwood High School he was the features editor of the paper and was critical of news commentators such as Walter Winchell, whom he believed interpreted rather than reported the news. At age seventeen he volunteered as a neighborhood civil defense officer, then spent a year in college before enlisting in the army air corps as a weather observer and serving in North Africa during World War II.

After the war he attended Stanford University on the G.I. Bill and earned bachelor's and master's degrees in political science. He blossomed as a college student and was elected to Phi Beta Kappa in 1948. He moved on to Harvard, where he earned another master's—this one in government—two years later, then returned to Stanford to attend law school in 1950. One of his classmates was Sandra Day O'Connor, who would eventually serve with him on the Supreme Court.

One professor was so impressed with Rehnquist's legal thinking and scholarly work that he arranged a private interview for a clerk's position with Supreme Court Justice Robert Jackson, who was visiting the law school to dedicate a new building in the summer of 1951. After the interview Rehnquist thought Jackson "had written me off as a total loss." Nevertheless, he was offered the highly coveted eighteen-month position.

It appears that Jackson, a moderate, had little influence on his clerk's political or judicial philosophies. In a book Rehnquist wrote in 1988 on the Supreme Court, *The Supreme Court: How It Was, How It Is,* he spoke well of Jackson but made no mention of any influence. In fact, Rehnquist wrote a memo to Jackson urging a continuation of the equal but separate decision when the Supreme Court was considering the *Brown vs. Board of Education* decision that eventually ended school segregation. When asked about it later during his confirmation hearings, he said it simply represented Jackson's thinking. But Jackson joined the unanimous decision ending school segregation.

After completing the clerkship, Rehnquist married Natalie "Nan" Cornell, whom he had met during his law school years, and in 1953 they moved to Phoenix, where he entered private practice. He said he chose Phoenix for its pleasant weather and favorable political leanings. The Rehnquists had a son, James, and two daughters, Janet and Nancy.

After a quiet five years, Rehnquist received some public notice when he was appointed special prosecutor on a case of alleged fraud concerning state highway contracts. He also began to participate in Republican Party activities, achieving prominence in the Phoenix area as a strong opponent of busing to achieve racial integration of schools. *Arizona Republic* reporter Dave Wagner said that Rehnquist was a segregationist who fought the passage of a Phoenix ordinance in 1964 permitting blacks to enter stores and restaurants.

In 1962 he was the leader of Operation Eagle Eye, a group of GOP lawyers that swept through polling places in south Phoenix to question the right of some minority voters to cast their ballots. At his confirmation hearing a decade later, Rehnquist testified he didn't recall doing such a thing. At his confirmation hearings for chief justice in 1986, he still had no recollection of the event and denied challenging any south Phoenix voters at the polls.

Manuel Pena, a Democrat and thirty-year veteran of the Arizona legislature, testified at the 1986 hearing that he had seen Rehnquist challenge individual black and Hispanic voters. The Senate Judiciary Committee probed Rehnquist's credibility in 1971 and 1986 but never established that he had committed perjury.

In 1971 federal judge Charles Hardy, a supporter of Rehnquist's appointment to the Supreme Court, wrote a letter to the chairman of the Judiciary Committee. It said:

> In 1962, for the first time, the Republicans had challengers in all of the precincts in this [Maricopa] county which had overwhelmingly Democratic registrations. At that time, voters could be challenged on whether they had resided within the precinct for 30 days before the election and whether they could read the U.S. Constitution in the English.
>
> In each precinct . . . every black or Mexican voter was being challenged on this latter ground, and it was quite clear that this type of challenging was a deliberate effort to slow down the voting so as to cause people awaiting their turn to vote to grow tired of waiting and leave without voting.

Pena recalled that at one precinct "the line was a half-block long, four abreast. Of six voting machines, only one was being used. They wanted people to become frustrated and leave." He said the precinct was 40 percent Hispanic and 90 percent Democratic.

It was legal to challenge voters as long as the challenger had probable cause to believe the voter was ineligible and the cumulative effect did not interfere in the voting process. The legislature prohibited such practices two years later.

Rehnquist campaigned for Republican presidential nominee Barry Goldwater in 1964. During that time he befriended another Phoenix attorney, Richard Kleindienst, who was Goldwater's national director for field operations.

When Kleindienst became a deputy attorney general in the Nixon administration, he recruited Rehnquist to work in the Attorney General's office as an assistant attorney general for the Office of Legal Counsel. Rehnquist defended the constitutionality of President Nixon's policies in Indochina, Nixon's orders withholding certain government documents, and the mass arrest of peaceful demonstrators. His backing of the administration's law-and-order program won the attention of Nixon, who was looking to appoint judicial conservatives to the high court.

During his early political years Rehnquist had characterized liberals sitting on the Supreme Court as "left-wing philosophers," including Earl Warren, William O. Douglas, and Hugo L. Black. He accused them of "making the Constitution say what they wanted it to say." Now one of his principal functions was to screen candidates for potential Supreme Court positions, along with Kleindienst and Attorney General John Mitchell.

Unable to find a suitable candidate to replace retiring justice John Marshall Harlan, Mitchell informed Rehnquist that he would be the nominee. Despite his relative youth (he was forty-seven), inexperience, and political views that diverged from those of many senators, his nomination was confirmed, 68 to 28, on December 10, 1971.

In his early days Rehnquist was outspoken as the Court's lone dissenter, despite the presence of three other Republican appointees. He battled against the expansion of federal powers and advocated a strong vision of state's rights. He also differed from the majority's view of the Fourteenth Amendment as it applied to nonracial issues such as the rights of women, children, and immigrants.

His dissents influenced very few of the Court's decisions, but he was setting the stage for the Court's future shift to a more conservative view. His opinions often reflected the position that the Court's liberal faction too often tried to shape public policy by expanding the scope of the law beyond its original meaning. Harvard law professor Laurence Tribe observed, "Even in lone dissent, he has helped define a new range of what is possible."

Rehnquist dissented in *Roe vs. Wade* in 1973, in which the majority based a woman's right to an abortion on a constitutional right of privacy. He wrote, "To reach its result, the court necessarily has had to find within the scope of the Fourteenth Amendment a right that was apparently completely unknown to the drafters of the amendment."

Professor David L. Shapiro wrote a sixty-four-page appraisal of Rehnquist's tenure in 1979 in the *Harvard Law Review* and concluded that the justice was guided by these three basic propositions:

- Conflicts between the individual and the government should be resolved in favor of the individual.
- Conflicts between state and federal authority should be resolved in favor of the states.
- Questions of the exercise of the jurisdiction of the federal courts should be resolved against such exercise.

By 1986 Rehnquist held significant persuasive power. After Chief Justice Warren Burger retired, President Reagan nominated Rehnquist to replace him. Liberals howled in protest. Many painted Rehnquist as a racist and conservative extremist. Senator Edward Kennedy, the Massachusetts Democrat, denounced him as having an "appalling record on race," and liberal columnists branded him a right-wing extremist. Opponents again brought up his activities in Phoenix. They were labeled as old charges, and no serious charges of misconduct were alleged about his fifteen years as an associate justice. In the end, the Senate confirmed Rehnquist by a 65 to 33 vote on September 17, 1986.

During the 1987 term he achieved a high level of agreement with his fellow justices, ranging from 57.6 percent with Thurgood Marshall to 83.1 percent with Anthony Kennedy. He also revealed a moderation in his views by voting to protect gay rights and free speech.

As chief justice, Rehnquist won respect through his efficient management of Court affairs. His managerial abilities in the 1987 term won the praise of Justice Harry Blackmun, who called him a "splendid administrator in conference." Said Harvard professor Richard Fallon, "As an administrator he is very firm—someone who absolutely keeps things on time. He wants things done in a timely, efficient manner."

Perhaps his influence is felt most through his use of the chief justice's power to assign opinions on cases in which he is in the majority. This is an important power because the justice who circulates the initial draft of an opinion, particularly in a sensitive case on which the Court is closely divided, is the one who frames the issue and defines the terms of the debate.

There is no doubt that during the last quarter of the twentieth century, Rehnquist amassed what is perhaps the most conservative record of any Supreme Court justice. He and the Court majority hewed to judicial restraint, a legal philosophy that interprets the Constitution narrowly, deferring to legislative outcomes whenever possible. In conflicts between federal and state authority, Rehnquist generally favored states.

He believed "the Constitution is not designed to provide for the resolution of our social problems, but only to ensure that when the political branches of government undertake such resolutions, they do so under certain limitation," noted Kenyon College professor Harry Clor.

He has maintained a historical and judicial interest in past impeachment proceedings. In 1992 he wrote *Grand Inquests,* a detailed account of the House impeachment and Senate trial of President Andrew Johnson and the proceedings conducted in 1804 for Supreme Court Justice Samuel Chase. Ironically, seven years later it was Rehnquist's responsibility to preside over President Clinton's impeachment trial. His role was limited, and his rulings could be appealed and overturned by a simple majority of senators. The trial went off without a hitch, and the chief justice was praised for the way he handled the proceedings.

Controversy was to stalk Rehnquist again in late 2000, when he ruled with the majority in the 5 to 4 decision that rejected a ballot recount of the disputed Florida election, letting George W. Bush's victory stand. The decision was criticized as a political rather than judicial one. Later Rehnquist said he hoped the U.S. court system "will seldom, if ever" become embroiled in another presidential election.

"Despite the seesaw aftermath of the presidential election, we're once again witnessing an orderly transition of power from one presidential administration to another," the chief justice said. "This presidential election, however, tested our constitutional system in ways it has never been tested before. The Florida state courts, the lower federal courts and the Supreme Court of the United States became involved in a way that one hopes will seldom, if ever, be necessary in the future."

A widower since 1991, Rehnquist now spends his free time engaged in quiet activities, such as oil painting, singing, stamp collecting, going to the theater, and playing poker.

Mo Udall

Once when Congressman Morris K. "Mo" Udall was playing golf, he was asked what his handicap was. "Handicap?" he replied. "Man, I'm a one-eyed Mormon Democrat from conservative Arizona. You can't find a higher handicap than that."

Such a handicap never seemed to get in the way of the 1976 presidential candidate and thirty-year member of Congress, who was one of the giants of the environmental movement in the twentieth century. From high plateau farm boy to member of the highest political circles in the nation, Mo Udall had an enormous impact on the nation.

It all started in the small predominantly Mormon town of St. Johns (population 1,400), in the northeast corner of Arizona. Born on June 15, 1922, Morris King Udall was the fourth of six children of Levi and Louise Udall. Working the land was a way of life that early on instilled conservation and environmental values in Morris and many other young people of St. Johns.

At age six Morris lost his right eye after a playmate accidentally cut it with a knife and a drunken doctor botched the treatment. The eye became infected and had to be removed to prevent loss of sight in the other eye. A year later Morris came down with life-threatening spinal meningitis.

He got into his share of mischief as a youngster. Once he took Brother Lillywhite's new flivver for a joyride. Lillywhite always parked his car on a hill so he could jump-start it by letting it roll downhill. While Lillywhite was in church, Morris and another boy took the car, but Morris missed a turn and ran it into an irrigation ditch. Only then did he realize that Lillywhite's eighteen-month-old daughter was asleep in the back seat. "I toiled for two long summers in the fields to pay off my fine," he said.

He excelled in sports, was editor of the school paper, was an actor in school plays and played in the marching and dance bands. He also was elected student body president. Even as an adolescent, Udall showed workaholic tendencies.

After high school he went off to the University of Arizona to study and play basketball, but the start of World War II delayed his education. He enlisted in the army and went to Officer Candidate School, then was assigned to administrative duties in the States.

The site of Udall's main tour of duty was an army training facility at Lake Charles, Louisiana. It was quite a cultural shock for a Mormon from the high desert of northeastern Arizona to move to the Deep South, where he was placed in charge of a black squadron. Because he had planned to go to law school, he was assigned to both prosecute and defend soldiers accused of crimes. One of those he defended was a black soldier accused of murder. The trial was a life-changing experience. Udall lost the case and the soldier was sent before a firing squad. For years he carried a newspaper clipping about the execution in his wallet.

As Udall was wont to do throughout his career, he took on the status quo while in the service, writing a letter to the American Veterans Committee in March 1946 urging desegregation of the army. It took until 1949 for President Harry S. Truman to end desegregation in the military. Udall was discharged from the army air corps as a captain eleven days after his twenty-fourth birthday and returned home to resume his schooling.

In those days students could attend law school without an undergraduate degree, and Udall enrolled in law school, played basketball for the University of Arizona Wildcats, and became student body president. He and brother Stewart also helped integrate the Coop, the school's only dining facility.

At the end of the 1947–48 school year, Udall played professional basketball for the Denver Nuggets while completing law school requirements at the University of Denver. His pro career lasted one year, and after earning his law degree, he returned to Tucson to open a law practice with his brother. He also found time on his twenty-seventh birthday to marry Patricia Emery, a young woman he had met at a Nuggets basketball game. The Udalls would have six children: Mark, Randy, Dodie, Anne, Brad, and Kate.

Stewart and Mo took just about every hopeless law case that came their way, often pulling off surprisingly big monetary judgments. Mo was elected county attorney in 1953. In 1954 Stewart sought one of the two congressional seats in Arizona, and Morris ran for superior court judge. While Stewart won and would serve three terms in Congress, Mo lost his race, primarily because his name was listed last alphabetically on the ballot. Many voters complained they could not find it. He returned to private practice and during this time wrote *Arizona Law of Evidence,* a book still widely used.

Then in 1961 President John F. Kennedy appointed Stewart secretary of the interior. That opened his seat in Congress. Mo jumped at the opportunity, defeating radio personality Mac Matheson by a narrow margin, and the Mo Udall family was off to Washington and a new life. Sporting a crewcut, bow tie, and wide leather belt studded with turquoise stones and fastened by a silver Navajo buckle, the six-foot-five Udall was easy to spot around the Capitol.

Once in Congress, he began to refine his stock in trade— humor. He kept four loose-leaf binders of jokes that he had saved over the years that he could call on for the right occasion. But much of his wit was spontaneous, often leaving his audience holding their sides in laughter or groaning over a story they had heard before. Udall often said that he did not need new jokes; he only needed new audiences.

In 1998 he wrote a book entitled *Too Funny To Be President,* which sold 15,000 copies. Udall preferred to use jokes to bring people together. "The best jokes," he said, "are those that succeed in making all of us laugh together—not at someone or some group or someone's religion. Done well, a good joke can always make us feel a little better—and one in poor taste, nothing can make us hurt worse. Good political humor is never cruel, ridiculing, or belittling."

Mo took over his brother's office and set out to learn about Congress and his colleagues, keeping a book of names and pictures so he could identify House members. He took up where brother Stewart left off by attacking the House seniority system of power, but with little success. In his view the strict seniority system was at the root of Congress's inability to solve some of the country's problems.

"Most congressmen, it appeared to me, seemed content to tolerate a process that rewarded longevity, not merit—and thus ensured mediocrity," he said. He joined the Democratic Study Group his brother had helped to form, which was made up of the young Turks in Congress, and within two years was a heavy hitter in House reform movements. Drawing on his own experience, he wrote his next book, *Job of a Congressman,* to help new lawmakers learn the congressional system.

In 1964 Udall thought about seeking Barry Goldwater's Senate seat when the Arizona Republican ran for the presidency, but there was no guarantee that Goldwater would win the nomination. It was possible he would return to Arizona to seek reelection. Udall said he decided against running because he loved the House, his wife was against it, and "besides, I've taken a poll, and Barry Goldwater beats the hell out of me."

In the mid-1960s Udall began his environmental efforts, serving on the Public Land Law Review Commission. The experience gave him valuable insight that he would use in later years when he sought legislation to protect millions of acres of wilderness, set aside scenic Alaska lands, create strip-mining laws, and tighten up mining laws. He also introduced a bill on population control, earning the title of "bravest man in Washington" from one lawmaker who noted that Udall had six children.

Pat Udall despised Washington, and suffering from rheumatoid arthritis, she returned to Arizona. Udall visited Tucson often, but the marriage was in serious trouble, and in January 1966 the couple divorced. Almost two years later Udall married Ella Royston Ward, a secretary of the postal subcommittee he chaired. It was Ella who changed Mo's mode of dress. With his sleek new swept-back haircut, long ties, and elegant suits, he more closely resembled what people thought a congressman should look like.

In 1967 Udall began efforts to change the accountability of House members by introducing legislation to limit campaign costs, provide federal funds for campaigns, require public disclosure of expenditures and contributions, and other campaign reforms. One of those reforms—public disclosure of personal assets, which Mo had been doing himself since 1964—brought outrage from his colleagues. Congress finally passed a major overhaul of campaign financing in 1971, the first since the Corrupt Practices Act of 1925. After Watergate, Congress made more improvements, passing the Campaign Finance Act of 1974, which Udall and Republican John Anderson of Illinois sponsored.

In the mid-1960s Udall began to have serious doubts about the U.S. involvement in Vietnam, which led to his break with the Johnson administration despite the fact that his brother was in Johnson's cabinet. On October 22, 1967, he gave what he called "one of the most difficult speeches of my career," coming out in opposition to the Vietnam War before a Tucson audience. He was one of the first in Congress to take such a bold and unpopular position. "Waiting for things to happen is not leadership, and steering a safe political course is not the highest order of public service," Udall said.

He also took a lead role in exposing the My Lai massacre in Vietnam, which was brought to his attention by a former soldier, Ronald Ridenhour, who had been told about it. At his urging, Udall persuaded the army to look into charges that U.S. troops were responsible for the mass slaughter of dozens of men, women, and children at My Lai. Udall said the letter from Ridenhour "saved our country from the guilt of a monstrous cover-up of the whole shameful My Lai affair."

One of the ways Udall attacked the seniority system was by rallying young liberals around him as he attempted to jump over more senior House members to assume control of the Democratic leadership. While others agreed that the seniority system was archaic, only Udall had the courage to go right for its throat.

"[Udall] understood that political death is not when you lose an election; political death is when you have the power to do something and don't do it," said David Obey, the Wisconsin Democrat. Udall decided to run against House Speaker John McCormack in 1969, but the timing was not right and he was soundly defeated. He tried for majority leader again in 1971 but fell far short. However, the stir he caused made the House leadership take notice, and slowly the seniority system began to crumble.

At the same time, he was helping push through the Central Arizona Project, the multibillion-dollar plan to bring Colorado River water to Phoenix and Tucson. Virtually from the day he entered Congress until he left office, he fought for construction and financing of the mammoth project, once remarking that he had spent more time on the CAP than on any other issue in his thirty years in the House. Toward the end, however, he wondered whether the CAP was an environmentally correct project to pursue, but he also knew that he would be voted out of office if he came out against it.

In another incongruity, Udall, an ardent liberal who supported the working man, voted against repeal of the right-to-work amendment of the Taft-Hartley Act because his constituents supported the right to work. Again he knew that if he voted to repeal the amendment, he would be out of a job.

He also sponsored the Postal Reorganization Act of 1971, which led to today's independent postal system. Once when asked about how he would control inflation, Udall poked a little fun at the postal system by remarking, "Maybe we ought to turn [inflation] over to the post office. They may not stop it, but they'll damn well slow it down."

His concern about the danger of ill-considered technological advancement prompted Udall to warn in 1972 that " 'growth' and 'progress' are among the key words in our national vocabulary. But modern man now carries Strontium 90 in his bones . . . DDT in his fat, asbestos in his lungs. A little more of this 'progress' and 'growth,' and this man will be dead."

The environmental community, he argued, needed to start tackling society's "gut, controversial issues," such as racial discrimination and unemployment. During the 1970s energy crisis he predicted that "most Americans will never see a wilderness area, park or wildlife refuge, and unless they are brought into the fold, when the crunch comes they can be expected to opt for power, light, and heat at any cost."

In 1976 Udall asked, "What kind of society, given the choice between recycling a mountain of paper and denuding a mountainside of trees, would make a decision to do the latter? The answer: our kind. And it is time to change that."

Despite his defeats for House leadership in 1969 and 1971, Udall had a new goal: the presidency. In what his brother Stewart called "audacity," Mo Udall announced in 1974 that he was going to run for the Democratic nomination for president from the unlikely spot of the House of Representatives. Only one or two House members had sought the presidency since James A. Garfield in 1880, and, said Udall, "He got himself shot."

On one campaign trip to New Hampshire, Udall came up with what may be the most-quoted vignette of the entire campaign. He said he walked into a barbershop and began introducing himself: "Hi, I'm Mo Udall and I'm running for president." "Yeah, we know," the barber replied. "We were laughing about that this morning."

Udall campaigned long and hard, but he was short of funds and the other candidates split the liberal vote, giving the moderate to conservative Democratic vote to Georgia Governor Jimmy Carter. Udall called himself a progressive rather than a liberal. Once when things were going poorly for his presidential campaign, he was asked if he would accept the second spot on the Democratic ticket. He replied, "I'm against vice in every form, including the vice presidency." Udall fell short again, but he picked up 1.6 million of the popular vote and was second to Jimmy Carter in delegate votes at the Democratic National Convention.

In the primaries he finished second in seven states. Reflecting on the losing campaign, he quipped, "The people have spoken—the bastards." It brought howls of delight from supporters. Udall entertained thoughts of running again in 1980 and 1984, but by then Parkinson's disease was taking a heavy toll on his health and he thought better of it.

After the 1976 election Udall was elected chairman of the House Interior Committee and turned the committee into a strong supporter of the environment. The long fight against the seniority system was beginning to pay off, as he would not have qualified for the chairmanship based on his seniority. In 1977 he led efforts to restore nearly 1.5 million acres of strip-mined land, an area larger than North Carolina, and in 1978 he was instrumental in getting Nuclear Regulatory Commission records opened to public scrutiny. He also helped secure passage of the wilderness preservation acts in 1984 and 1990, which set aside 3 million acres of wilderness in Arizona. And he pushed through legislation preserving 104.3 million acres of Alaskan land.

Udall was hated in Alaska for his conservation efforts, but years later Alaskans began to see the benefits of setting aside the land, primarily the tourism it fostered. When Udall returned to Alaska several years after the legislation, he remarked, "Times have changed for my coming up here. I think I'm doing better now. When people wave at me, they use all five fingers."

Mark Van Putten, president of the National Wildlife Federation, said that passage of the Alaska Lands Act in 1980 was "a monumental moment in American history, and Mo Udall deserves a lot of the credit for it."

Udall also was an ardent supporter of the rights of Native Americans, a crusade that he passed along to John McCain when he was elected to Congress in 1983. McCain has carried the ball for Indian rights since Udall left office. One of Udall's long-time aides, Frank Ducheneaux, a member of the Cheyenne River Sioux tribe, noted, "There were too many political headaches and no gains for the senior members [to help the Indians], so Mo did it. It was a liability to westerners and of no benefit to eastern members."

His colleagues in 1980 rated Udall as the second most respected House member, third most persuasive debater, and the most effective committee chairman for getting legislation through Congress. He was approached about becoming commissioner of Major League Baseball and the National Basketball Association, but neither possibility came to fruition.

By the early 1980s Parkinson's disease was taking a toll on Udall's health. It had been diagnosed in 1977, but he had been able to carry on, although at a diminished capacity.

His second wife, Ella, committed suicide on August 13, 1988, and a year later, on August 6, 1989, he married Norma Gilbert, a former Capitol Hill lobbyist he had known for several years. Seventeen months later Udall was hospitalized when he fell backward down some steps at his home and slipped into a coma from which he never recovered. While he was in the hospital, brother Stewart wrote a poem entitled "Elegy at a Brother's Bedside."

> Like the hawks he knew as a boy
> His spirit soared and darted there.
> And now, crushed, we see him supine,
> His face fixed in an empty gaze.
> Our vigil is to no avail.
> Gone is the wit which sped the dance of laughter,
> Gone the lambent lacework of the mind.

What savage civility impels us to prolong "life" when the fight for life is over?

When will we allow loving hands to close lives that have closed?

Mo Udall resigned from Congress on May 4, 1991 (his wife Norma was allowed to submit a letter of resignation for him). After nearly eight years in a coma, he died on December 12, 1998.

In his honor Congress established in 1987 the Morris K. Udall Fund for Excellence in Public Policy at the University of Arizona and in 1992 the Morris K. Udall Foundation, which works on environmental and Native American issues. It is only the fourth congressional foundation ever established. The other three honor Barry Goldwater and Presidents Harry Truman and James Madison.

President Clinton awarded Udall the Presidential Medal of Freedom in 1996. One of his sons, Mark, went on to become a congressman from Boulder, Colorado, where he joined Stewart Udall's son, Tom, a congressman from New Mexico.

Lorna Lockwood

She looked like everybody's grandmother, but Lorna Lockwood was a pioneer for women in the law, rising to chief justice of the Arizona Supreme Court and twice being a candidate for the U.S. Supreme Court. From the days when she was only the second woman to graduate from the University of Arizona Law School, through her years struggling to practice law, and finally to her time as the first woman in the nation to sit on a state supreme court, Lockwood was a mentor for hundreds of women lawyers who followed her.

Lorna Elizabeth Lockwood came by her early interest in the law through her father, Alfred, a lawyer who also rose to a seat on the state supreme court. She was born on March 24, 1903, in Douglas, Arizona, a community on the Mexican border that also produced two U.S. ambassadors—Lewis Douglas and Raul Castro. Her father was the city attorney until he was elected to the superior court in Cochise County and they moved to Tombstone, the notorious "Town Too Tough to Die," in 1913.

"I recall that I used to go down to my father's law office and I used to think how wonderful it would be if I could some day practice law with him," she told historians Mildred and Abe Chanin. "Father thought that was interesting but he had an idea that girls should learn housekeeping." With eight other students, she graduated from Tombstone High School in 1920, where she had been in the school band, played the cello, and been on the basketball team. The family lived in a modest one-story, three-bedroom, wood-frame house with no indoor plumbing that was situated across the street from the courthouse.

In 1920 Lorna went off to the University of Arizona in Tucson to study. She worked for the school newspaper, winning an award as outstanding reporter. She also belonged to the Riding Club and the girls' track team, and was one of the founding members of the Chi Omega social sorority.

Her father insisted she live in a dormitory, North Hall, so she would get good grades. She completed her degree in three years, with a major in Spanish and a minor in psychology. Her father had arranged for her to take law courses while she was an undergraduate to be certain that the law was what she truly wanted. When she showed that it was, her father gave his blessing and she enrolled in the University of Arizona Law School, despite efforts by the school's dean to discourage her. "He said it was no place for a woman," Lockwood recalled. She was one of thirteen students in the first-year class; forty were enrolled in the school.

"So, I went into the law school and I was very timid," she said. "After all, I was the only girl in the class, and remember that this was right after World War I, and there were a lot of returning soldiers and they were considerably older than I." She told the Chanins, "As it turned out they were very nice. They took me just as I was, and I was just another student."

She was elected president of the Student Bar Association. When she graduated as the second woman from the law school, she said about the dean, "I think he was proud of me."

It would be fourteen years before Lockwood would practice law. There were few jobs for women lawyers in those days. Female attorneys usually worked for title companies, in the trust departments of banks, or for the government. She wanted to work with her father, but by then he had been elected to the state supreme court.

So she worked as his secretary and law clerk for seven years while he sat on the supreme court, where she doubled as a law clerk. During that time she was a Democratic precinct committee woman and the president of the Democratic Women's Club, and was active in the Order of Eastern Star and the National Federation of Business and Professional Women's Club. In 1932 she formed a partnership with another Arizona Law School graduate, Loretta Savage, in a small room in the Luhrs Building in Phoenix. It was the first all-women law partnership at a time when only five women were practicing law in the city. Most of their cases were minor ones, referred to them by more successful attorneys. They agreed to split up in the spring of 1942 because they were making no money.

In 1938 Lockwood ran for the state legislature and won, serving two two-year terms. Only three or four other women had preceded her in the legislature. But there were five other female members of the house when she was elected—Maxine Brubaker, Nellie T. Bush, Laura McRae, Louise Moore, and Claire Phelps. Lockwood decided against seeking a third term, bowing out to help in the war effort. She became a Washington secretary for Arizona Congressman John Murdock, a former professor at Arizona State in Tempe, where she had taken a summer class from him as an undergraduate.

Lockwood returned to Phoenix in 1944 to become a price attorney for the U.S. Office of Price Administration. In 1945 she joined her father, who had lost a reelection bid for the supreme court, and her brother-in-law, Z. Simpson Cox, in private practice. In 1947 she was again elected to the state legislature, where she served until her appointment as assistant attorney general in 1949. Like many women before and after her, working as an attorney for the government was one of the few avenues open to her. In late 1950 she was elected to the superior court bench in Maricopa County, becoming the first woman to hold that post. Fourteen candidates sought five openings on the bench. She finished fourth.

"People were surprised," she told the Chanins, "but the lawyers were the ones that were a little bit against it. They didn't think a woman belonged on the bench. One of them said he knew I was a good lawyer, but he just didn't believe women should become judges. After I was elected, he changed his mind and we became very good friends. There weren't any valid reasons given, just that a woman hadn't been there and shouldn't be."

In 1954 she took over the juvenile bench, where she was considered a tough but excellent judge. She was devoted to children. "My hobby, my only hobby, is children," she once said. "I think you might even call my hobby my first profession." She never married because, she said, her career or her marriage would, in the end, suffer, and she was not one to do things halfway.

Also not one to utter empty words, Lockwood put her devotion to children into action. While on the bench, she was active in Campfire Girls and the Big Sisters and Big Brothers of Arizona, and she helped establish the Girls Ranch of Arizona, a residential treatment center for troubled girls.

About her service on the juvenile court, Lockwood said:

I have always believed that the juvenile court, as well as every other court, has a twofold purpose—to protect human rights and to enforce human responsibilities. The juvenile court should consider not only the best welfare of the individual child brought before it but should also consider what is best for other persons including parents and society with which the child may be in conflict. I have always felt that parents bear a great responsibility, and the court should always attempt to make a juvenile court proceeding a truly family affair, involving not only the child, but also the parents. My general juvenile court philosophy is that we should give more time, energy and financial support to get a juvenile back on the road to good useful citizenship than we do adults. The main reason for this is that a young person may more easily be turned into the right direction and we as society just do not have either the time or the money to try to rehabilitate all persons who have turned aside from the path of good citizenship.

Nonetheless, the job as juvenile judge was stressful, and it began to affect Lockwood's health. She moved back to the regular bench, where she stayed three more years. During that time she became the first woman in Arizona to sentence a man to death. When she told the man that he must die for his crime, she swallowed hard, bowed her head, and told him, "May God have mercy on your soul." In 1960 she decided to run for the state supreme court. It had always been her ambition to follow in her father's footsteps.

A fellow attorney and close friend, Virginia Hash, was a pilot and flew Lockwood around the state to campaign. She would fly to such faraway places as Ajo or Kingman in the evening and then fly back in the morning to resume her duties on the bench.

She was the only candidate for her first term because the incumbent, M. T. Phelps, withdrew at the last minute. When she won, she moved into Suite 227 in the state capitol, the same office her father had occupied. In subsequent elections she faced opposition. The first year she was on the court, she served with Levi Udall, the father of Morris and Stewart. In her fourteen years on the bench, she would issue more than five hundred opinions, gaining the respect of her colleagues, who selected her for a term as chief justice.

Lockwood's terms were marked by her belief in the equality of all people before the law. She was particularly proud of her ruling that allowed a woman to sue for damages if her husband had been injured or disabled. "It had never been that way," she told the Chanins. "We had to overturn one of the laws that said a man could ask for damages but a woman could not. I saw no reason why the law shouldn't work both ways." She also ruled that a Native American who had been elected to office and had been denied certification could hold the office. "I held that since the United States had made the Indians citizens they had the right to run for office and had the right to election." When she supported the Equal Rights Amendment before the Arizona legislature, she was outspoken on women's rights, as usual. She said men were opposed to the ERA because they thought it would make women less feminine. "And I can't see that at all. I don't think that when I served on the Supreme Court I was any less a woman. And in my own intellectual capacity I had no question of femininity or masculinity. I was a judge, a judge of the Supreme Court."

She once wrote a prayer that she said guided her on the bench. It was called "A Judge's Prayer."

I pray that today I will have the knowledge to discover and the wisdom to clarify the legal issues; the ability to see, and the unbiased mind to recognize the true facts; the heart to know, and the gentleness to understand the human problems; the patience and logic to reach, and the courage to declare the just decision. All these things, Lord, I ask that at the close of this day my conscience may truly say, "I am worthy to be a judge."

One of the state's most powerful lawyers, John Frank, said, "Throughout her whole life and her whole career, in marked and very special degree, Lorna Lockwood has possessed the quality of legal creativity. In a tradition-encrusted profession in which novelty is not the order of the day, she has never been afraid of an idea because it was new."

She believed that Americans should be knowledgeable about the political process. "I am concerned with the indifference of the great number of Americans who seem to feel no pride in our heritage of freedom nor any sense of duty to make even small sacrifices of time and energy to take an active part in choosing, encouraging and supporting honest, strong and intelligent leaders to preserve that freedom." Those are words that still ring true today.

She taught a class in politics for women at the Phoenix downtown YMCA. In 1971 she was one of three women who traveled throughout Arizona trying to interest people in the Action Course in Practical Politics, which was sponsored by the National Federation of Business and Professional Women's Clubs. Its purpose was to "show people how they can take part in politics in every way, from licking envelopes and knocking on doors to running for office."

In a ruling on a divorce case, Lockwood wrote, "Our decision in the case rests on public policy. The obligations of marriage cannot be thrown aside like an old coat when a more attractive style comes along."

While serving on the state's highest court, she was considered twice by President Johnson for a seat on the U.S. Supreme

Court, in 1965 to replace Arthur Goldberg and in 1967 to replace Tom Clark. Her recommendation came from Senator Carl Hayden. But Johnson appointed Abe Fortas to replace Goldberg and Thurgood Marshall to replace Clark. She would say that the position should go to the most qualified judge, regardless of sex. "I don't think a woman should be denied a seat on the court just because she is a woman and I don't think she should be given one just on the basis of being a woman either. The job is too important to be judged on this basis alone. I think the United States benefits by having the very best qualified people—whether man or woman."

She resigned from the state court in September 1975 at the age of seventy-two and returned to private practice. A diabetic for many years, she had a number of small strokes before dying of pneumonia on September 23, 1977.

Carl T. Hayden

If Arizona's first senator, Henry Ashurst, was a show horse, his colleague in the upper chamber, Carl Hayden, was a work horse. In his fifty-seven years in Congress—forty-three in the Senate and fourteen in the House—Hayden went quietly about his work, earning a reputation as one of the shrewdest, most powerful politicians in the country.

From the day he showed up in Congress in 1912 as a frontier sheriff to his last day on the floor as a bent, withered figure of ninety-one years, Hayden was a respected legislator. "Never give your enemies any more reason than they already have to go on hating you," he once said.

Throughout his career he exhibited a concern for natural resources. President John Kennedy said at a testimonial dinner for Hayden, "Every federal program which has contributed to the West—irrigation, power and reclamation—bears his mark. And the great federal highway program which binds this country together, which permits this state to be competitive east and west, north and south—this in large measure is his creation."

Los Angeles Times reporter Jerry Cohen once wrote, "He has assisted so many pet projects for so many senators that when old Carl wants something for his beloved Arizona, his fellow senators fall all over themselves giving him a hand. They'd probably vote landlocked Arizona a navy if he asked for it."

He was known as the "silent senator." As fellow Arizonan Morris Udall said, "Perhaps he achieved so much because he was a doer, not a talker." Hayden was found of saying, "When you have the votes, don't talk." Associated Press reporter Arthur Edson wrote in 1966, "In a temple dedicated to windbaggery, he has kept his mouth shut while astutely pushing out invisible tentacles of power."

He learned to keep quiet not long after he was elected to the House. After he had given a speech, one of his fellow congressmen remarked: "You just had to talk. Every word that you said was taken down by that reporter. It will be printed in the *Congressional Record* and you can never get it out. There are two kinds of congressmen—show horses and work horses. If you want to get your name in the newspaper be a show horse, but if you want to gain the respect of your colleagues, keep quiet, be a work horse and speak only when you have the facts." He took the words to heart. When he was honored for fifty years of service in Congress, it was noted that his remarks in the *Congressional Record* consumed less space than those of any other senator serving at the time.

One time Jack Kennedy, then a young senator from Massachusetts, tried to strike up a conversation with Hayden, asking him what the difference was between the Senate of that year and the one thirty years earlier. Hayden chomped down on his cigar and replied, "Young men didn't talk so much then."

Carl Trumbull Hayden was born on October 2, 1877, at Hayden's Ferry, along the Salt River—later to become Tempe. He was the first white child born in the Phoenix suburb. He and his sisters, Sallie and Mary, attended a one-room school. He was healthy but puny. "Carl was born before germs were invented," Sallie would say. He made a horseback trip alone into the Grand Canyon when he was fourteen, traveled alone to Mexico City for sightseeing, and when he was sixteen, took the train to Chicago to see the World's Fair. Said his father, "If he can't take care of himself at this age, it's high time he was learning."

Carl attended public schools and the normal school, which later became Arizona State University, then went to Stanford University from 1896 to 1900, where he studied economics. He arrived at the university wearing a cowboy hat and corduroy trousers. "I lived in Encina Hall and nobody paid any attention to me," he would say years later. "After some time, I wrote to my mother saying that if she wanted her boy to look like other boys she would have to send me some money. When it came, I went to San Francisco, where I obtained skin-tight pants, high roll-down collars, and all the other things that a young man then should wear." After changing attire, he received invitations to visit fraternity houses but turned them down. "I remained a 'barbarian' so long as I was a member of the student body."

One classmate he befriended was Herbert Hoover, later to be president of the United States. (Hayden would be awarded the Herbert Hoover Medal for Distinguished Service in 1967.) He managed to get his weight up from 130 to 180 pounds by the time he graduated, heavy enough to make second string on the football team. When his father died in 1900, he had to drop out of Stanford and return home.

"I could have played center on the first Rose Bowl team," he said. "But I thought it was more important to come home for the Christmas holidays than play some Eastern team." Not that he would have made much difference. Stanford lost to Michigan 49 to 0.

His father had operated a mercantile and flour-milling business in Tempe that was in financial difficulties. So when Hayden returned home, he entered politics, a calling that paid a decent living. He served on the Tempe town council from 1902 to 1904 and was a delegate to the Democratic National Convention in 1904, where he stood on a chair while announcing that Arizona cast its four territorial votes for William Randolph Hearst, the newspaper baron. He was elected Maricopa County treasurer in 1904.

At Stanford he had met Nan Downing, "the most beautiful girl that ever lived." They were married on Valentine's Day in 1908 and honeymooned at the Grand Canyon. He called her "Pal" and she called him "Bug." They had no children.

That same year he was elected sheriff of Maricopa County, which included Phoenix, a town of about 10,000 inhabitants. But he was not a traditional Wild West sheriff. "I never shot at anyone and nobody ever shot at me. About the nearest I ever came to shooting was the day I identified a horse thief who was supposed to be badly wanted in Utah, Colorado and Wyoming." Hayden found the man in a bar, stuck his gun in his back, and took him to jail. When the three states refused to pick him up, Hayden set him free, on the promise he would not steal any horses in Arizona.

Once he was called to run down two train robbers who had escaped on horseback. Hayden sent Indian scouts after the suspects while he commandeered an Apperson Jackrabbit, an automobile of the times, and set out in hot pursuit. The bandits were no match for the galloping Indians and the chugging Apperson and were quickly captured. Nan Hayden worried about the dangers of chasing train robbers, but her husband assured her, "There was no danger. I couldn't have hurt them, for my rifle had no cartridges in it. I never carry a loaded gun." When he went around to collect fees for the county from gambling operations, he was often invited to take a drink. "I would explain that I had a rule— nothing before sundown."

In those days the state was heavily Democratic, and Republicans were considered carpetbaggers. That changed in the 1950s when a young Phoenix city councilman, Barry Goldwater, began turning the state into a Republican stronghold. But there was no question which party Hayden belonged to when he ran for office. In the first state elections held in 1911, he was chosen as Arizona's first member of the U.S. House of Representatives and served in that chamber through March 3, 1927. During his first campaign the *Phoenix Gazette* remarked, "Carl Hayden will make the best Congressman that Arizona will ever send to Washington. A man of sterling character, sound convictions and dominating personality, Hayden will make himself known in the halls of Congress. . . . Hayden is a born fighter and he will not allow the interest of the new state to be overlooked." He received 11,556 votes in the statewide race, while his Republican opponent, Jack Williams of Tombstone, earned 8,485. Women and Native Americans were denied the vote then.

Hayden became known as the "service congressman" who faithfully answered constituents' mail and inserted packets of flower and vegetable seeds in his letters. He would often say how undressed and strange he felt in his early days in the House without wearing a gun.

In 1912 he supported Democratic nominee Woodrow Wilson and went to bat for him over the League of Nations. That same year he introduced his first bill, authorizing construction of a railroad to Fort Huachuca, a historic frontier cavalry post and now a major U.S. Army post. He and three colleagues defied an executive order forbidding members of Congress to volunteer for military service during World War I, and he was sent to Camp Lewis, Washington. He ended up a major in the U.S. Army during World War I, serving as a battalion commander.

He was a sponsor in 1919 of the legislation extending the right of suffrage to women, and cosponsored the bill that created the Coolidge Dam as well as the Hayden-Cartwright Bill, which provided for the beginning of the federal highway system.

He was the sponsor and floor manager of the bill that established the Grand Canyon National Park. Hayden's language inserted in the legislation creating the Boulder Canyon Project, where the Hoover Dam now sits, was extremely important to the basin states of Arizona, Colorado, Nevada, New Mexico, Utah, and Wyoming. It limited the amount of water that could be taken by California out of the Colorado River. That language would be important years later when the U.S. Supreme Court ruled in Arizona's favor on water entitlements from the Colorado.

In 1926 George W.P. Hunt, a seven-term governor, heard that Hayden was considering a run for the Senate. Hunt ordered him not to run because he wanted the job himself. Hayden marched into Hunt's office and told him, "George, I got your orders. But I'll run against you and beat the pants off you." Hunt realized that Hayden was right and decided against running. Hayden defeated incumbent Republican Senator Ralph Cameron by a vote of 25,918 to 17,980 in the general election and served six six-year terms, until January 3, 1969, when he retired from office.

In 1939 he sponsored legislation authorizing government-insured loans to farmers—the Farmers Home Administration. He warned early of the threat of Nazism. He argued on the Senate floor against cuts in military appropriations and argued for new military installations and warships and for increasing the size of the army. After the war he helped fellow Arizona Senator Ernest McFarland to secure passage of the G.I. Bill of Rights.

During the late 1940s and early 1950s, because of its two senators, Arizona had far more clout than any other state for its size. McFarland was majority leader of the Senate during the Truman administration, and Hayden had served twenty-five years and was chairman of the Senate Appropriations Committee. Between them they had forty-four years of seniority.

In a tribute to Hayden on his fiftieth anniversary in Congress in 1962, Mo Udall said, "This man knows the legislative processes as few others have learned them. He knows that legislation is compromise, he knows that there must be give and take, and he knows how legislative work is accomplished." But Hayden was not so sure. With typical modesty he remarked on the CBS television program *Washington Conversation,* "Oh, I don't think anybody fully understands it yet. There are all kinds of angles to it. There is always something new turns up."

Democrat Senator Strom Thurmond of South Carolina noted at the Hayden tribute, "No other man has had the distinction of serving this long in Congress, and I venture to say it will be a long time before another does." It turned out Thurmond broke Hayden's record of serving in the Senate; by 2001, at the age of ninety-eight, he had served forty-six years in the Senate. But no one has topped Hayden's total of fifty-seven years in the House and Senate.

Despite the fact that in the early 1950s Arizona took a conservative turn, Republican leaders were reluctant to take on Hayden. They recognized the value of his Senate seniority. In 1962 Republican leaders Barry Goldwater, Paul Fannin, John Rhodes, and Bob Pickrell agreed that Arizona would suffer if Hayden were defeated, especially because he was chairman of the Appropriations Committee, important to the state's effort to fund the Central Arizona Project. Evan Mecham won the

Republican primary to oppose Hayden, but he got little or no help from the Republican Party. In the end Hayden won by 36,000 votes. On the Saturday before the election, Hayden had to stop rumors that he had died by getting out of his bed at the Bethesda Naval Hospital and holding a news conference to show that he was indeed alive—not well, but alive. His wife, Nan, had died in 1961 after fifty-three years of marriage.

One of the projects that Hayden worked hardest for was the Central Arizona Project, a dream that he nurtured from the 1920s. He was fighting for the CAP right up until the bill was signed in 1968. "He has displayed a capacity for work that a man half his age could be proud of," Mo Udall said. On his ninetieth birthday in 1967, he was still setting a stiff pace. Aides used to complain that the senator worked from 9 A.M. to 6 P.M., seven days a week. In 1968, when President Lyndon Johnson signed the legislation creating the CAP, he remembered that on the day he was sworn in as a senator in 1949, Hayden "propositioned me about the Central Arizona Project."

Hayden was president pro tempore of the Senate from 1957 until he left the Senate in 1969. That put him third in line for the presidency. Asked whether he would take the presidency if it ever got down to him, he replied, "I'd call Congress together, have the House elect a new speaker, and then I'd resign and let him become president." In his last thirty years he was a member of the Appropriations Committee, serving the final fourteen years as chairman.

Toward his final years in the Senate, Hayden usually had a cigar in his mouth and still enjoyed a glass of his favorite bourbon. He used his cane to wave people onto elevators, and he had hearing loss. He would greet senators way past Social Security age with an "All right, Sonny." He often boasted that he had all of his teeth but two. In his last years in the Senate, he walked every day from his apartment to the Capitol one and a half blocks away.

In 1968 Goldwater was planning to seek the Senate seat he had given up when he challenged Lyndon Johnson for the presidency in 1964. His opponent would have been Hayden. A poll taken in January of 1968 showed that Goldwater would defeat Hayden 46 percent to 42 percent, but 12 percent of voters were undecided. Goldwater liked Hayden and knew he stood a chance of losing the race. However, Hayden knew that Goldwater could beat him and thus humiliate him in the last years of his life. He decided to retire.

Hayden had secured passage of the Central Arizona Project, so his work was essentially done. In his retirement announcement he said, "Among the other things that fifty-six years in the House and Senate have taught me is that contemporary events need contemporary men." He also said, almost sobbing, "Well, the Old Testament has said it best, so I will use it in modified form to close: 'There is a time of war, and a time of peace, a time to keep, and a time to cast away, a time to weep, and a time to laugh, a time to stand, and a time to step aside.'"

He spent his final years at work on his papers in the Arizona State University's Hayden Library, named after his father. He read the Senate summary in the *Congressional Record* daily and scanned the newspaper. He was glad to be home. "I never liked the climate in Washington," he said. "I don't like cold weather. It can't compare with the nice climate we have back here."

He died on January 25, 1972.

Raul Castro

Raul Castro—judge, governor, and U.S. ambassador to three Latin American countries—was a native-born Mexican who faced racial discrimination at almost every stop along the way of his political and legal career. "Basically, my career has been based on dreams, on ideology, on the basis that I wanted to achieve something that hadn't been achieved for the benefits of myself and somebody else, my people, I guess," he once said.

As a youngster Castro said he once heard a man who called himself "the Old Walrus" speak at the Tenth Street Park. "Good people of Douglas," he said. "I'm glad to be here. Who knows, one of these days one of these barefooted kids here may be your next governor." And he pointed toward Castro. The man was George W.P. Hunt, Arizona's first governor. Later, of course, Castro would become governor and that city park would be named after him. It was across the street from the Elks Club, which banned Mexicans from membership. Later a park and recreation center in Cananea also would be dedicated to him by the state of Sonora.

Raul Hector Castro was born on June 12, 1916, in Cananea, Sonora, Mexico, a town fifty miles south of Bisbee. His father, Francisco Dominguez Castro, had been a deep-sea diver in San Jose del Cabo in Baja California before moving to Cananea to become a miner. He never attended school. His mother, Rosario Acosta, had a third-grade education and taught her husband how to read and write. Castro's father was ordered out of Mexico because of his involvement in a Cananea mine strike. He had been sent to prison but was released as a political refugee. He and his wife and twelve children came to Arizona. Two more were born in the United States.

The Castro family lived about five miles from Douglas, in Pirtleville, where 98 percent of the residents were Mexican. Raul's father loved politics and would read to him from prominent Mexican newspapers. "I was bored to death," Castro said. He wanted to go play with other children, but his father wanted him to absorb all the current events. "So that's, I think, where my first exposure to political life was, through my father." When Raul was twelve or thirteen years old, his father died, leaving fourteen children. His mother became a midwife to support her family.

Douglas schools were segregated, and Raul went to the Fifteenth Street School, which was strictly for Mexican youngsters. Mexicans were thought of as "dirty and dumb," Castro said. School buses would pass by him and his friends, and the Anglo kids would wave at them out the windows. There was no bus for the Mexican children, so they walked to school, regardless of how far it was. Before-school activities included a game called Race-Against-Race. The Anglos would line up on one side of the playground and the Mexican kids on the other. "We'd put rocks in our fists and we'd sock and hit and kick and bite and chew, anything went. By the time we went to class, we were all bloody and dirty and sweaty and what have you, and the schools tolerated it."

The Mexican children were forbidden to speak Spanish in school. In fact, if a student got caught, the teacher would whack him or her on the hand with a stick. "Well, by the time we got home my hands looked like baseball mitts," Castro said. He was a quarterback on the high school football team and competed in track, and he was a good student.

Segregation was not just in the schools. Mexican children were banned from using the YMCA swimming pool except on Saturday afternoons. "They cleaned out the pool in the afternoon," Castro said. "So right before they cleaned out the pool, that's when we could go swimming. By that time the pool was dirty and slushy. I looked at the sign, YMCA. I said, 'What's Christian about this situation?' I didn't see anything Christian about it."

Raul had no middle name, and at the time of his graduation from Douglas High School in 1935, he realized that every Anglo student had a middle name. An embarrassed Castro told the principal his middle name was Hector, the name of a school basketball player who was his idol. "What a horrible name. I could have done better than that, I think."

Although Raul was a good student, his high school principal tried to discourage him from attending college, saying that "frankly you're wasting your money and time. Nobody will hire you, as you well know, on the border. We don't hire Mexican kids and it's impossible to place you. So why go [for] higher education if it's not going to be of service to you?"

Despite the admonition, Castro earned a football scholarship to Arizona State Teachers College (now Northern Arizona University), which had about 475 students. A condition of the scholarship was that he wash dishes three times a week. He eventually worked his way up to assistant cook. He also became captain of the boxing team—never losing a collegiate fight as a middleweight—and taught a sixth-grade class in Flagstaff. (He would say later that nothing in his career had given him greater satisfaction than teaching at the elementary school level. "So when I identify with myself, I always identify with being a schoolteacher with young people. I wasn't crazy about university students because I think by that time it's a little late.")

After graduation he returned to Douglas hoping to become a teacher. A school official told him he was a "great guy" but was not going to be hired. "[The school board is] not going to hire any Mexican American kids to teach school in Douglas," the official said. What his high school principal had told him was proving true. He became a naturalized citizen at the age of twenty-three.

"I was very bitter to think that I was coming back and thought I was going to be the football coach or something, or be able to do something in my own hometown." The hard-jawed, barrel-chested Castro hopped a freight train out of town and began boxing professionally for about fifty dollars a bout. "The fortunate part is that these bumps that I had in my life have been good to me; I think they made me charge ahead." The discrimination he experienced, he said, "more or less molded my life and motivated me to try to improve relations between peoples of different parts of the world."

After barnstorming for a year and a half, Castro returned to Douglas, where he got a job with the State Department in Agua Prieta, Mexico, handling immigration work for about five years. He left when he was told, "A Mexican with a Spanish name does not have much chance to advance." He quit to attend law school at the University of Arizona at the age of twenty-eight, and he taught Spanish at the university to pay for his education. When he applied to the law school, Dean Byron McCormick told him he would have to quit the teaching job because law school would be too difficult for him. Mexican Americans have a language problem and "they just are not able to do it," McCormick said.

Castro complained to the university's president, Alfred Atkinson, who told McCormick, "Let Castro enroll. Let him prove his worth. If he can't do it, well then flunk him." Castro kept his job and eventually graduated in 1946. He opened his law practice in an old, rickety two-story building at 199 North Church Avenue in Tucson. He lived in a room "in the back, cooked in the middle and had my office in front." The "shingle" hung in front of the building was a fraternity paddle with the handle chopped off. It said, "Raul Castro, Attorney at Law." His first clients were poor and often left tortillas as payment.

While practicing law, he earned a seat on the YMCA board of directors in Tucson. "Then I was able to try to modify the policy of the YMCA, and I did," he said, referring to the exclusionary tactics from his Douglas days. In those days private attorneys also could serve as deputy county attorneys, so he also worked in the Pima County Attorney's office under Bob Morrison. Mo Udall was the assistant county attorney and later became the county attorney. When Udall decided to run for superior court judge, Castro entered the race for county attorney. He was elected by sixty-five votes and served from 1954 to 1958.

"I recall crossing the street in Tucson going to [the] Valley National Bank and three cowboys were going down the road, and as I was walking I was campaigning. One told the other guy, 'I'd rather vote for a dog than for a Mexican.' He wanted me to hear it. I went, 'Woof, woof.' All I wanted was their vote. And I got elected. Talk about a thick skin. That's a thick skin, I think—it hurt."

At the age of thirty-eight Castro married Patricia M. Steiner, who was a deputy U.S. marshal. The couple would have two daughters, Mary Pat and Beth. Patricia was an Anglo, but she learned firsthand about the discrimination faced by Mexican Americans. Whenever she and Castro visited Phoenix overnight, he would send her ahead to get a hotel room because no one would rent to him.

In 1958 he ran for superior court judge and was elected, becoming the first Mexican American in the state to hold such a position. He was still battling discrimination in those years. Once when he was living along the Rillito River in Tucson, he was painting a fence around the yard while wearing boots, a straw hat, and Levis. A Border Patrol car drove by and an agent asked him for an immigration card, which he said he did not have. Then the agent asked for whom he worked. "La señora," he replied. They were about to put him in the car when Castro pointed to a sign on the gate that said, "Castro Pony Farm." The agent asked him if he was Judge Castro, and Castro replied that he was. "Oh, geez," the agent said and drove off.

In 1964 U.S. Senator Carl Hayden urged President Johnson to appoint Castro as an ambassador. Johnson refused because he worried that Castro would be confused with Raul Castro, the brother of Cuba's revolutionary president, Fidel Castro. He asked Hayden if Castro would change his name. Castro told Hayden, "No. This is the name I came to this world with. I don't intend to change it just to be a diplomat."

Hayden prevailed and Castro was appointed ambassador to El Salvador, where he served for four years. He was to be known as the "Yankee Castro" so no one would mistake him for the Cuban dictator's brother. For his service El Salvador presented him with its highest honor—the Matias Delgado Decoration. Later he became ambassador to Bolivia for two years. There he was known as the "Ambassador on Horseback" because he rode into the countryside to greet Bolivians. Twice his home at the embassy was bombed by terrorists. When Richard Nixon became president, Castro was removed as ambassador and returned to Arizona to run for governor.

He said he decided to seek the governorship because all his life he had heard that Mexican Americans couldn't achieve their dreams. "I had the feeling that it could be done, that I could do it. So for me it was a personal thing. I also felt, naively or otherwise, perhaps I was on my white horse and charger, but I felt I could do something on behalf of the Hispanic community."

On June 18, 1970, Castro announced he was entering the Democratic primary against auto dealer Jack Ross of Phoenix and Chandler mayor George Nader. When he held a news conference in Tucson to announce his candidacy, no one showed up. "They thought it was crazy. There's no way I could run for governor and get elected. So they weren't interested. Nobody appeared."

He drove to Phoenix to hold another news conference, this one at the Westward Ho hotel. Three people attended. He wasn't deterred. He had little money and campaigned by stopping people in the street to ask for their votes. "I always felt the American public prefers an underdog. If you're an underdog and give the American public a chance, they'll support you. . . . And I think you've got to believe in yourself." That underdog, as the *Arizona Republic*'s Bernie Wynn put it, was enhanced by "a color of speech, a sparkle to his personality and a charm to his appeal." Castro won the Democratic primary and in the general election faced Republican Jack Williams, who was seeking his second four-year term.

Republicans claimed that Castro had been a somewhat indifferent prosecutor as Pima County attorney, showing favoritism to defendants of Mexican extraction, and that he had been an adequate but not outstanding judge. But the Republicans decided not to attack Castro's record for fear they would be accused of picking on a member of a minority. Williams's campaign manager, Steve Shadegg, called it "an error I came to regret." Castro had no hesitancy in attacking Williams. And the Republicans had to combat the poor-boy-makes-good legend surrounding Castro.

The race eventually pitted the entire state against Maricopa County, where Williams had his main support. Castro exploited that division of state politics. But in the end Williams prevailed by 9,000 votes, a 50.9 to 49.1 percent victory.

When Williams decided against running again in 1974, five Republicans lined up for the job, including perennial candidate Evan Mecham and the eventual Republican nominee, Russ Williams, no relation to Jack Williams. Businessman Russ Williams had served two terms on the Arizona Corporation Commission. Castro faced two Democratic opponents, winning the primary with twice as many votes as his opponents combined.

The bitter primary battle among the Republicans badly split the party. In addition, Castro attacked the previous administration and the Republican-controlled legislature. He also had the support of labor, which in 1974 still carried a great deal of clout throughout the state. Because of his close race the first time, the Hispanic community had confidence he could win.

"They walked the streets, they rang doorbells, and I can tell you they took deep pride in the fact that I was running for governor of Arizona," Castro said. He defeated Williams by 4,119 votes, becoming the state's fourteenth governor. The margin of victory apparently came from the Native American vote in Navajo and Apache Counties, where the turnout on the reservation was the largest in state history. He received 5,488 votes more than Williams in those two counties. Castro carried with him a majority in the state senate, 18 Democrats to 12 Republicans, but lost the house to Republicans, who outnumbered Democrats 33 to 27.

Castro was sworn in on January 6, 1975. He was only the second governor ever elected from Pima County. The first, Sam Goddard, served one two-year term from 1965 to 1967.

Castro was criticized by the Republican establishment virtually from the day he took office. Said columnist John Kolbe of the *Phoenix Gazette,* a strongly pro-Republican newspaper, "Covering the amiable and peripatetic chief executive has become a newsman's jungle of half-completed sentences, imprecise factual data, and even contradictory assertions." Some claimed that all Castro wanted was to be a governor, not to act as a governor.

The governor played a strong role in helping Jimmy Carter carry Arizona in 1976 and also campaigned for him in Texas and New Mexico. Apparently Castro was frustrated by his battles with the legislature and weary of the bad press, because when Carter offered him an ambassadorship to Argentina in 1977, he jumped at it and resigned, turning the governorship over to Secretary of State Wes Bolin, the next in the line of succession.

"I searched my soul [about resigning] with a feeling that [the Hispanic community] worked so hard for me, they were so proud of me. . . . That's the cross I had to bear and it bothered me and there's no question about it." But he said he felt he could be of better service to the country as ambassador to Argentina than as governor.

Castro even experienced a form of discrimination in Argentina. He told Ernest Calderone, an oral history interviewer from the bar association, that the Argentines were angry over his appointment. They questioned why America would send a "Mexican" as ambassador. "After all, they are a European country," Castro said. "And they didn't want a Mexican as an ambassador. They wanted a lily-white, freckled-face, Anglo-type individual." But he persevered and stayed until 1980 before returning to Arizona.

After his retirement from government service, Castro returned to his first love—teaching. He often visits schools throughout the state at his own expense and on his own time to motivate children. "They look at me and they say, 'Why, gosh, you look like I do. You look like one of us.' I say, 'Yes, I'm one of you.' And give them the feeling that they can do it, that it can be accomplished, it can be done. Get them away from the defeatist attitude."

He also travels the world and specializes in immigration law. Since 1995 he and his wife, Pat, have made their home in the border city of Nogales, Arizona.

Fife Symington

"Arizona, the Scandal State."

The headline screamed off the page of the June 24, 1996, issue of *Time.* How did the magazine reach that conclusion? Republican Governor Fife Symington had become yet another embarrassment to the Grand Canyon state.

Failed real estate dealings have relegated Symington to the company of former Governor Evan Mecham, savings and loan king Charles Keating, and several state legislators caught up in

Azscam, the 1991 bribery sting concerning approval for a non-Indian gambling casino in Arizona.

"[Symington] told people he would run Arizona like a business," state Democrat chairman Sam Coppersmith told *Time*. "Every Arizonan has been praying that he didn't mean like his business."

After a five-year federal investigation, Symington was indicted in 1996 on twenty-three felony charges, ranging from making false statements to wire fraud, in regard to his real estate developments in Phoenix during the 1980s. He went from two-term governor to restaurant pastry chef in a matter of six years and eventually won a pardon from President Clinton on the president's last day in the White House. How did it all come to this?

John Fife Symington III was born on August 12, 1945, in New York City and raised in Maryland. His great-grandfather was the nineteenth-century steel baron Henry Clay Frick, who made a fortune in his association with steel magnate Andrew Carnegie. Symington attended Harvard, where he supported Barry Goldwater for president in 1964 and received a bachelor's degree in Dutch art history in 1968. Having completed ROTC training at Harvard, he was commissioned a second lieutenant in the air force and spent four years in the service, including fourteen months in Vietnam in 1970–71, for which he was awarded a Bronze Star. He was a weapons controller and was involved in search and air rescue. By the time he mustered out of the air force in 1972, he was a captain.

Like many newcomers, Symington moved to Arizona after being introduced to the state while in the military. He had been stationed for a period at Luke Air Force Base in Phoenix. After his tour of duty, he moved to Phoenix with his wife, Leslie Barker Symington, in 1972 and took a job with the Lincoln Property Company. That same year, at the age of twenty-seven, he was appointed to a seat on the Southwest Savings and Loan board of directors. At the end of the year, his wife filed for divorce. They had two sons, John IV and Scott.

Three years later he married Ann Olin Pritzlaff, heiress to the Olin Corporation fortune. A prenuptial agreement kept their estates separate. They had two sons, Richard and Thomas, and a daughter, Whitney. In 1976 he left Lincoln to start the Symington Company, building warehouses in Phoenix. He also became politically active, serving as a Republican precinct committee member and winning a two-year term as the party's state finance chairman.

In September 1983 the Southwest board approved a partnership with Symington to purchase a twenty-acre site for the Camelback Esplanade, an upscale office, retail, restaurant, and hotel complex. The savings and loan, with Symington abstaining, voted to put $30.5 million into the property as an "equity investment" rather than as a conventional loan. Symington was later accused by federal authorities of violating the rules for federally insured institutions by failing to get their approval of the transaction and failing to get an appraisal of the property. The next January, Symington left the board, he said, to avoid a possible conflict of interest over the investment.

Symington remained politically active throughout the 1980s. At one point he urged Governor Mecham to resign from office when he faced impeachment, recall, and criminal charges in 1988. At the same time Symington was the chairman for former Congressman John Rhodes's campaign to replace Mecham in the 1988 recall election. The recall election was never held, however, because Mecham was impeached and removed from office by the state legislature.

Southwest was declared insolvent under the weight of $941 million in bad loans and investments on February 27, 1989. The Federal Deposit Insurance Corporation seized the Esplanade and began an investigation of Symington's activities.

Symington noted that all savings and loans in Arizona had gone under during that period except one small one in Glendale. "Nobody can regret more than I do the failures of Arizona's [savings and loan] institutions," Symington wrote in an *Arizona Republic* article. "A lot of hardworking Arizonans have been hurt by the disaster and are still suffering." But he also became defensive. "Unfortunately, there are people who for political reasons relish the opportunity to inflict more suffering."

Then Symington's political ambitions got bigger, and in April 1989 he announced his candidacy for governor. Although he campaigned on his business expertise and his success as a real estate developer, he refused to answer questions relating to the details of his businesses, which were beginning to gain attention because of their financial instability. "What Arizona needs right now is a business mind," he said as he began his election campaign. "The state needs a man who can provide experienced, professional fiscal management to pull it out of its economic crisis. I am that man."

He won the Republican gubernatorial nomination, defeating four other candidates, including former Governor Mecham and former Congressman Sam Steiger. In the general election he narrowly won the popular vote in a three-way race but failed to get the required 50 percent of the vote. As a result, he had to face Democrat Terry Goddard, a former Phoenix mayor, in a runoff election.

Goddard warned voters that Symington could be indicted for his business activities, while Symington retorted that the congressional hearings on the failure of Southwest Savings were scheduled during the election campaign as "a blatantly partisan attempt to interfere with Arizona's gubernatorial runoff." Despite the investigation, Symington won on February 28, 1991.

Less than three months later Symington unveiled a plan to cut the size of government, dubbing it Project SLIM, State Long-

Term Improvement Management. Charges of rigged bidding over the contract for a private company to operate SLIM soon surfaced.

Fourteen companies had submitted bids, with Coopers & Lybrand the highest at $1.9 million. Nonetheless, the accounting firm became one of five finalists and eventually reduced its bid to $1.46 million, still the largest. Price Waterhouse's bid was $874,828. Six of eleven members of the selection committee chose Coopers & Lybrand, saying its bid reduction was "extraordinary."

Later it turned out that a Coopers & Lybrand partner, John Yeoman, was working double duty as Symington's personal accountant. Yeoman was accused of talking with George Leckie, a Symington aide, about the bidding process. Two Symington aides told the governor that Leckie may have leaked information to Yeoman and Coopers & Lybrand. Leckie denied the allegation. In March 1994 Symington asked Maricopa County Attorney Rick Romley to investigate. Romley found no criminal wrongdoing, nor did state Attorney General Grant Woods. But Coopers & Lybrand agreed to a $725,000 settlement with the state, admitting a "grave appearance of impropriety," and agreed to stay out of the state contract business for two years.

Then a federal grand jury indicted Leckie and Yeoman on charges of defrauding the state of more than $1.5 million by rigging the Project SLIM bid. Less than a month later Yeoman was killed in a Phoenix car wreck two days after pleading not guilty. Leckie was eventually acquitted on all charges.

Less than a year after Symington was elected, the Resolution Trust Corporation sued him and eleven other former directors and officers of the failed Southwest Savings and Loan for $197 million, alleging they did not seek appropriate regulator approval for the Camelback Esplanade. The amount was later raised to $210 million.

In February 1992 the U.S. Attorney's Office in Los Angeles

took over a criminal investigation of Symington's finances. In May 1993 the governor ran into more personal problems when the Mercado, a retail and office project that he had developed in downtown Phoenix, was auctioned off for $3 million, leaving him $7 million in the red because he had personally guaranteed the construction loan. In February 1994 the Esplanade, which had cost more than $200 million to build, was sold at a trustees' auction for $70 million.

The Resolution Trust Corporation suit was settled in May 1994 for $12.1 million, but Symington still denied any wrongdoing. Six months later he was reelected, despite the federal investigation and his collapsing development empire. He defeated Democrat Eddie Basha, a grocery chain owner.

Fourteen months later a Maricopa County Superior Court judge ordered Symington to pay back more than $11 million to six union pension funds that had helped finance the Mercado. Three months later the governor filed for personal bankruptcy, citing debts of more than $24 million and assets of $61,000. Thirteen of his projects went belly up. Despite the bankruptcy, Symington's lifestyle changed little, thanks to his wife's inherited fortune, which was protected from the bankruptcy proceedings.

Symington's troubles got worse. On June 13, 1996, a federal grand jury indicted him on twenty-three counts, alleging he had repeatedly lied about the value of his crumbling real estate empire to obtain credit and had used the governor's office to try to get out of a $10 million loan.

"The days of secrecy and innuendo and endless leaks are over," he told a news conference. "At long last the day in court is now near." He predicted he would be acquitted and said he had no intention of resigning as governor—an irony, considering that he had urged Mecham to step down when he faced criminal proceedings nine years earlier.

Symington was seeing a larger conspiracy in society. At a news conference, he called the press, the courts, and the universities "the three amigos of the anti-culture," responsible for all of society's difficulties, including his. "All around us," he said, "forces are moving to replace society's enduring values with new values. Selfishness over sacrifice; entitlement over enterprise; comfort over courage."

Symington's criminal trial began on May 13, 1997, and lasted for fifteen weeks. The jury had deliberated for eleven days when a seventy-four-year-old juror, Mary Jane Cotey, was dismissed because fellow jurors complained she was inattentive, confused, and unable to focus on deliberations. The next day an alternate juror replaced Cotey, who told reporters she had been "railroaded" off the jury because she would have voted to acquit Symington.

After nine and a half days of deliberation, Symington was convicted of seven counts of fraud. He resigned from office the next day and was succeeded by Secretary of State Jane Hull, also a Republican. In January 1998 one of the conviction charges was dismissed, and in February Symington was sentenced to thirty months in prison and five years' probation. The sentence was delayed pending an appeal.

The convictions were overturned two years later when the Ninth U.S. Circuit Court of Appeals ruled that Cotey was unfairly dismissed as a juror during deliberations. Said Symington: "I have never been afraid of anything. In this instance, I feel I have always been innocent. It was just a matter of time before we would prevail." And, he said, he would not seek a plea bargain to avoid a new criminal trial. "I don't think you ever compromise your principles," he said.

The civil case to recover the $10 million that Symington had borrowed from the six union pension funds to build the Mercado, plus $8 million in interest, continued into early 2001.

Then came the stunning announcement that President Clinton had pardoned Symington. Speculation arose that the pardon was granted because Symington might have saved Clinton from drowning when they were both in college, Symington at Harvard and Clinton at Georgetown, in the late 1960s. They had been attending the same beach party in Massachusetts when the rescue occurred. Clinton was swimming about a hundred yards offshore when he began struggling with a riptide. Symington rowed out in a boat to pull Clinton aboard. Years later Clinton remarked, "If it weren't for Fife Symington, I wouldn't be here."

Symington downplayed the incident. "I think the issue here is a little more profound than that. I think that both the incoming president and the outgoing president understand that we are entering a period of reconciliation. The hope is that people in public life are going to lower the rhetoric, not use the justice system for political ends, just try to calm the environment down . . . and I would view my pardon as part of that."

Later a lifelong Symington friend, Thomas Caplan, a Baltimore novelist who attended boarding school with the former governor and was Clinton's former college roommate, confirmed he had discussed the pardon with Clinton. Caplan said he was visiting Clinton in the White House on December 19, 2000, and asked about a possible pardon. Clinton responded, "He should apply." Symington said, "I was really shocked, surprised and happy that he asked me to submit." Symington's attorney, John Dowd, said the pardon application was not submitted through the Justice Department but went directly to the White House.

Symington called it "the most elegant way to end this saga" and said that it was a "magnanimous" decision. He called it a "pre-emptive pardon, because as things stand right now, I'm not convicted of anything. But I have openly admitted many times that I've made some mistakes. Where I differed with the group that went after me was that there was never any criminal intent, and frankly, there was no financial harm [because of the Southwest and pension fund dealings] that I caused. What happened wasn't worth the kind of war that was declared on me."

Despite his denial that he would not seek a plea bargain, the

Arizona Republic reported on the day the pardon was announced that Symington was ready to plead guilty to one felony count of fraud to avoid another lengthy criminal trial if federal prosecutors agreed not to recommend jail time. Symington declined comment, saying, "It's all confidential . . . but it's all over. I'm free." He revealed that his wife had spent $5 million on his legal fees.

William Carlson, the foreman of the jury that found Symington guilty, said the pardon showed that there's justice for the wealthy and powerful but not for the less fortunate. "I feel like I've been kicked in the gut," he told the *Arizona Republic*.

While Symington no longer faced a possible prison term, the civil case proceeded. Symington ultimately got off rather lightly on his dispute with union pension officials. In September 2001 he agreed to pay $2 million to satisfy their $17.6 million bankruptcy judgment against him. He told them that if they didn't accept that, he would disinherit himself from money he would receive from a family trust, thereby denying the union any money. Symington stands to receive one-fourteenth of the estate of his uncle, Henry Clay Frick II, who is in his early 80s. In the end, Symington said his legal woes cost him about $15 million.

Symington has worked as a pastry chef since his graduation from the Scottsdale Culinary Institute, which he attended to fulfill a longtime interest in cooking. He has talked of opening his own cooking school.

Richard Kleindienst

Richard Kleindienst was only the second Arizonan to achieve a cabinet post when he was appointed attorney general by President Nixon in 1972. But his tour of duty was short-lived. It is commonly believed that Kleindienst was deeply involved in the Watergate scandal, but in reality he may have done as much as any other cabinet member to ensure that Nixon was brought to justice. Regarding the misconception, his daughter, Anne, a Phoenix attorney, told the *Arizona Daily Star* after he died, "I think that's unfortunate because it was such a small part of his life. He just found himself caught up in it because of the others around him."

That is not to say he was innocent of other wrongdoing. After he resigned—some say he was forced out—Kleindienst returned to private life. But he was found guilty in 1974 of a perjury misdemeanor charge over testimony he gave during his confirmation hearings.

Before he left for Washington, he had been an important player in Arizona politics during the rise of Republican power in the 1950s.

Richard Gordon Kleindienst was born on August 5, 1923, to Gladys and Alfred Kleindienst near Winslow, a brown dirt plateau town in the northeast corner of the state, at the southern tip of the Navajo reservation. Winslow was a division point of the Atchison, Topeka & Santa Fe Railroad, for which Alfred Kleindienst worked as a brakeman when a young man.

Richard learned about Republican politics at the side of his grandfather Joe Kleindienst, a strict disciplinarian of German stock. His political work led to the appointment of Richard's father as postmaster in Winslow under Presidents Harding, Coolidge, and Hoover. Despite his Republican politics, Joe Kleindienst was a good friend of Democrat Carl Hayden, who served in Congress for fifty-seven years. Because of that friendship, Richard Kleindienst said Hayden was the only Democrat for whom he ever voted for federal office.

Kleindienst spoke fluent Navajo, an extremely complex language, thanks to the Navajo woman who raised him after his mother died of an infection following an operation. In the hours before his mother died, she told Richard, then fourteen, "Hitch your wagon to a star, Dickie, and if possible, someday try to go to Harvard." He did both of those, joining up with Barry Goldwater after he graduated from Harvard.

During his boyhood Kleindienst delivered the *Albuquerque Journal* to subscribers at 4:00 A.M. on below-freezing winter days. He was elected student body president in his senior year at Winslow High School, defeating the captain of the football team by one vote. He graduated in 1941, an undistinguished thirteenth in a class of fifty-five.

After two years at the University of Arizona, Kleindienst left to join the army air corps and served in Italy. When he returned, he enrolled at Harvard College and graduated magna cum laude, then earned a law degree from Harvard in 1950. While still at college, in 1948, he married Margaret Elizabeth "Marnie" Dunbar. They would have four children: Alfred, Wallace, Carolyn, and Anne.

Kleindienst returned to Arizona with his wife, passed the bar exam, and went to work for the firm of Jennings, Strauss, Salmon & Trask in Phoenix. He and Marnie joined the Maricopa County Young Republicans organization, where they met young men who would change the fabric of Arizona politics. Among them was the so-called "Arizona mafia" of Barry Goldwater, Howard Pyle, who would become governor, and John Rhodes, who would later serve thirty-two years in the U.S. House.

Pyle was elected governor in 1950, an event that helped arouse the moribund Republican Party in Arizona after decades of Democratic domination. The mood of the country also was changing, with Richard Nixon rising to fame in the wake of the Alger Hiss affair, Joe McCarthy grabbing headlines with his Communist witch hunt, and war hero General Dwight D. Eisenhower ascending to the presidency. Goldwater, who was serving on the Phoenix City Council, agreed to take on Democratic Senator Ernest McFarland, who was the Senate majority leader during the Truman administration.

Democratic registration in Arizona was six to one over the Republicans, so most people thought Goldwater's chances were slim. One of the reasons the Democrats outnumbered Republicans in voter registration was because of "Pinto Democrats," Republicans who registered as Democrats so they could vote for conservative Democrats in the primary election.

Goldwater managed to pull off one of the biggest upsets of the national 1952 election by defeating McFarland, who boasted of being one of the most powerful politicians in Washington. With Goldwater came other Arizonans into political prominence, including Rhodes and Kleindienst. The young attorney ran for the state legislature with the approval of his law firm, which gave him little chance to win a district where the registration was 4 to 1 against him. But, along with Goldwater, he rode Eisenhower's coattails to victory and at the age of twenty-nine became the youngest member of the Arizona legislature.

Before the 1952 election the Arizona house and senate were dominated by Democrats. After the election thirty-five Republicans were serving in the ninety-member house, a marked increase. But Kleindienst served only one term because his law firm pressured him to return. In 1954 two veteran members of the Republican Party—Jim Beaman and Dick Fennimore—called on Kleindienst to tell him he was going to be elected chairman of the Republican Party in Arizona. "You've got to be kidding," Kleindienst said. They responded, "Barry wants it, so shut up and do what you are told." And it was done.

Although the Republicans took a licking in the 1956 presidential election, they bounced back in 1958 with the reelection of Goldwater, Rhodes, and a new governor, Paul Fannin.

In 1964 Kleindienst was picked as national director of field operations of the Goldwater for President Committee, which helped Goldwater win the 1964 Republican presidential nomination. When told he was going to do the job, he asked, "What the hell's that?" Goldwater told him his job was to get 665 delegates to vote for him on the first ballot. Kleindienst replied,

"Barry, you've got to be crazy!" to which Goldwater responded, "You're right, Dick. If I weren't nuts, I wouldn't be doing this!"

Kleindienst resigned during the campaign to return home to run for governor against Democrat Sam Goddard. He lost, calling it "the screwiest experience of my life." Although shrewd and politically savvy, Kleindienst just did not have the magnetism of his mentor and friend Goldwater. In addition, he and Evan Mecham, who would be a perennial candidate for public office, became embroiled in a bitter personal race. Mecham had won the Republican nomination for the U.S. Senate in 1962 but lost badly to Carl Hayden. He thought about running for Goldwater's Senate seat in 1964 but chose instead to seek the governorship.

Mecham divisively attacked the Republican Party "bosses" who backed Kleindienst. Kleindienst beat Mecham by a 2 to 1 margin, but the bitter primary hurt him. He lost to Goddard by 30,000 votes at a time when a number of other Republican state and federal candidates won easily. After the election Kleindienst swore to himself that he was through with politics. That was not to be.

In 1966 he directed Jack Williams's successful bid for the governorship. Then in 1968 he accepted Nixon's request to become a regional chairman and get delegates for Nixon's 1968 run for the Republican nomination for president. Kleindienst had known Nixon since 1956, when he was Republican Party chairman in Arizona and helped the Eisenhower-Nixon ticket carry the state.

During the 1968 campaign Kleindienst drafted a detailed plan that helped Nixon win the Republican nomination. Nixon never forgot his effort. It was during that campaign that Kleindienst struck up a relationship with campaign chairman John Mitchell, who would become Nixon's attorney general. Kleindienst agreed to become a deputy attorney general.

Four years later he became attorney general when John Mitchell left the office to head CREEP, the Committee to Re-elect the President. In his autobiography Kleindienst modestly said, "I may be the only person to have attained the high position of attorney general of the United States for no other reason than my involvement in the organizational politics of the Republican party." He would last less than a year.

Kleindienst was sworn in as attorney general just five days before the Watergate break-in at the Democratic National Committee offices on June 17, 1972. He was playing golf when one of the Watergate burglars, G. Gordon Liddy, phoned to warn him that the burglars were in the pay of the reelection committee. Rather than try to block any investigation, Kleindienst ordered a full inquiry into the matter.

He remained attorney general only until May 25, 1973, resigning because he said he didn't want to lead a Watergate investigation. Upon his resignation Nixon said that Kleindienst had asked to be relieved of his duties because he felt a Watergate inquiry "may implicate individuals with whom he has a close personal and professional relationship." Kleindienst said he never again spoke with Nixon.

The mark that remains on Kleindienst's otherwise clean record was his guilty plea to a 1974 misdemeanor charge unrelated to Watergate. He admitted that he hadn't testified "fully and accurately" before a Senate committee during his confirmation hearing that Nixon had asked him to drop an antitrust case. He was given a suspended sentence of thirty days in jail and a $100 fine.

At the time he said, "I was wrong in not having been more candid with the committee and I sincerely regret it. It is my earnest prayer that in due time history will record that in [the antitrust case] the Department of Justice fulfilled its charge fairly to enforce the laws of the United States without fear, interference or favor." He said he pleaded guilty "out of respect for the criminal justice system of the United States and the indisputable fact that the system must have equal application for all."

In 1978 the *Washington Post* reported that Watergate special prosecutor Leon Jaworski had prepared an eight-count felony charge against Kleindienst over his testimony during his confirmation hearing but dropped the matter after meeting with Kleindienst's lawyers.

Kleindienst returned to Arizona and resumed his private law practice. In 1981 he was accused and acquitted of twelve counts of perjury concerning his legal representation in a 1976 insurance company fraud. The Arizona Supreme Court later suspended him from practicing law for one year, finding him guilty of two of nine disciplinary charges. He resumed practicing law in Tucson before moving to Prescott in 1996.

He died on February 1, 2000, after a four-and-a-half-year battle with lung cancer.

John Rhodes

When John Rhodes was a young attorney in 1950, he received a telephone call from Barry Goldwater. Rhodes had heard of Goldwater but had never met him. Goldwater was a Phoenix city councilman who was backing radio personality Howard Pyle, a Republican, for governor.

Goldwater asked Rhodes to run for attorney general, explaining that he was trying to put together a slate of Republicans to challenge the Democrats' dominance in Arizona. Rhodes replied, "Mr. Goldwater, there's something you should know. I don't want to be attorney general." Goldwater responded, "Well, Mr. Rhodes, there's something you should know. You won't be." Said Rhodes, "Well, with that understanding, I'll run."

At the time there were 225,000 registered Democrats and 50,000 Republicans in Arizona. Rhodes lost badly, getting 35 percent of the vote against Fred Wilson, but his vote was higher than that of most other Republicans. It was the last race Rhodes would lose.

Two years later, in the wake of Eisenhower's sweep into office and Goldwater's upset of Senator Ernest McFarland, Rhodes defeated longtime Congressman John Murdock. It started him on his way to succeeding Gerald Ford as House minority leader in 1973.

John Jacob Rhodes was born on September 18, 1916, in Council Grove, Kansas, and educated in public schools there. As a youngster he visited Washington, D.C., where he met President Calvin Coolidge and sat in the gallery of the House of Representatives. "I was more than impressed," he wrote in his autobiography, "and I thought that one day I would like to become a congressman and play a role in governing our country."

In high school he was elected president of the freshman, sophomore, and senior classes and as a senior was elected president of the student council. After graduating from Kansas State College in 1938 and Harvard Law School in 1941, he served five years in the army air corps during World War II. One of his posts was Williams Field in Chandler, Arizona. "I was a non-flying officer. One of my first duties was to organize the officers' mess. I hadn't learned anything at Harvard Law School to prepare me for that, but I did it." While in the service, he married his wife, Betty, in 1942. They would have four children: John J. ("Jay"), Tom, Elizabeth, and Scott.

After the war the couple settled in Mesa, where Rhodes began practicing law. Although he was interested in politics, Arizona was so dominated by Democrats that his chances for any political career seemed slim to none. Stephen Shadegg wrote in *Arizona Politics: The Struggle to End One-Party Rule* that Rhodes found out just how futile it was to be a Republican.

He went to register to vote in Chandler at the office of the justice of the peace. The justice saw that he was starting to fill out the form and asked, "Democrat, of course?" Rhodes said, "No, Republican." The justice looked up and said, "Are you sure you know what you're doing? This is a Democratic state. Your vote won't count if you're a Republican." Rhodes responded, "Well, Mr. Justice, my father may turn over in his grave for a lot of things, but this isn't going to be one of them." Rhodes said the justice then muttered, "I don't know whether this old machine can type that bad word, Republican!" Rhodes told Shadegg that he remembered that only twelve Republicans were registered in the Chandler precinct.

One reason there were so many Democrats was that many Republicans registered as Democrats so they could vote in the Democratic primaries, which is where the eventual winners were chosen. Those Republicans were given the name Pinto Democrats.

The Republican Party began to show life around the end of the 1940s when thousands of young men like Rhodes, who were stationed in Arizona during the war, decided to make the Grand Canyon state their permanent home. In 1950 Republican Howard Pyle won the governor's seat by beating state auditor Ana Frohmiller, primarily because she was a woman but also because there were more Republican voters. Pyle turned out to do an excellent job as governor, sending a message that perhaps other Republicans could govern as well.

In 1952 Republicans persuaded Rhodes to seek one of Arizona's two congressional seats. He was to take on John Murdock, a popular incumbent who had served sixteen years and was chairman of the Interior Committee, important to the state's water interests. Despite his position, Murdock had been unable to get the politically popular Central Arizona Project bill out of his committee.

Rhodes ran with the slogan "Ike needs me!" It worked. He rode Goldwater's and Eisenhower's coattails to victory, becoming the first Republican congressman from Arizona. He soon won over his Republican colleagues in the House. During the second year of his first term, he was elected president of the Eighty-Third Club, named for the eighty-third session of Congress. It was an organization made up of Republican freshmen in the House.

Rhodes was appointed to the House Interior Committee, where he would play a role in securing passage of the CAP. Because he had defeated Murdock, he said he "felt a great responsibility to get myself into a position to be effective in getting the Central Arizona Project authorized and financed." He never regretted his backing of the CAP, despite later misgivings by the Udall brothers. "The water is more expensive than we had hoped, and therefore it is used more by municipalities and industry than agriculture. [The CAP originally had been proposed to bring water to farmers.] But it is there, more valuable than gold in a thirsty land such as ours."

Rhodes called the 1960s the "Golden Age" of Arizona's representation in Washington. Joining him at various times were Senators Carl Hayden, Barry Goldwater, and Paul Fannin; Representatives Mo Udall, Bob Stump, and Eldon Rudd; and Secretary of the Interior Stewart Udall. Regardless of party affiliation, they all worked together for the benefit of Arizona.

One of the few votes Rhodes wished he had not made was in favor of the Gulf of Tonkin Resolution, which enabled President Johnson to enlarge the war in Vietnam. Like a great many other members of Congress, he had failed to read the resolution closely and had no idea it would give the president such broad discretionary authority to wage war in Southeast Asia. "It was one of Lyndon Johnson's successful manipulations of the Congress on the Vietnam war issue, which later proved to be his undoing."

In his autobiography Rhodes found fault with the decision to fight a limited war in Vietnam. He believed the United States would have won the war had the military been turned loose. The failure to confront the war head-on appeared to be deliberate. "The effect was to downplay the Vietnam war effort so it would not endanger President Johnson's domestic spending programs, the 'Great Society.' 'Guns and butter' we called it." Rhodes also put a share of the blame on Congress: "Congress ignored the issue until it was too late, and then tried to intervene in a destructive way, motivated primarily by partisan positions."

Rhodes began moving up the House chain of command, and his power began to show when he got into a power struggle in 1965 with newly elected minority leader Gerald R. Ford of Michigan. Ford had replaced Charles Halleck of Indiana, whom Rhodes had backed. Ford wanted one of his supporters to become chairman of the Policy Committee, the fourth in line of succession for Speaker of the House, but Rhodes was unanimously elected. That committee, comprising twenty-five to thirty House members, helped establish party positions on congressional matters. Later, on December 7, 1973, when Ford was appointed vice president to replace Spiro Agnew, Rhodes took his place as minority leader virtually without opposition.

Rhodes was considered a member of the conservative wing of the Republican Party, but in his later years his position was usually one of moderation. When he replaced Gerald Ford as minority leader, it was a difficult time for the Republican Party, with the Watergate scandal revelations at their peak. Rhodes had given President Nixon the benefit of the doubt but now began to be troubled. As minority leader he had to steer a middle ground between those who wanted to abandon Nixon and those who were loyal to him.

"One of my deepest concerns was to try to limit political damage to the Republican House members because of 'guilt by association.'" (Several months earlier Rhodes said he had a dream during which he and Goldwater urged Nixon to resign.) Nonetheless, he urged a prompt investigation by the House Judiciary Committee. Later, on what he called the saddest day of his life, he would join Goldwater and Senator Hugh Scott of Pennsylvania to confirm to Richard Nixon that he would be impeached and removed from office. They told the president all but twenty-five House members would vote for impeachment and that the Senate would overwhelmingly vote to convict. The next day Nixon told House and Senate leaders he would resign.

Goldwater said about Rhodes, "He willingly let others grab the spotlight and the headlines while he labored quietly and effectively to get things done. Moreover, he exhibited a rare capability of bringing warring factions together to achieve common goals."

Political columnist George Will said, "One glance tells you: God had a congressman in mind when He made John Rhodes. And he is just what the Founding Fathers had in mind when they designed the House of Representatives, the body intended to be closest to the common man."

Rhodes has been described as colorless, "shorter than average and heavier than he ought to be," and "a man who dresses in business suits that are almost flamboyantly nondescript." Will said, "His name is not a household word, and never will be. To his credit, he probably doesn't mind a bit." He wore a crewcut until he was fifty-six years old. Then one day he said to himself while looking in the mirror, "John, you're beginning to look like a fifty-six-year-old who is trying to look like he is thirty-six." So he let it grow out.

In 1976 Rhodes wrote *The Futile System,* a critical view of congressional operations. It was the outcome of his years of frustration "battling the unyielding majority." Forty years of Democratic rule in Congress, Rhodes said, had produced ineptitude and irresponsibility in the House.

Rhodes began thinking about leaving the House in the late

1970s when House members were divided on what direction they should take. He also realized that he wanted to accomplish other things in his life outside Congress and that his age "was such that I had better get out and begin it." Nevertheless, he was chairman of the Republican National Conventions in 1976, when Gerald Ford was nominated for a full term, and 1980, when Ronald Reagan was selected.

Discontent with the House leadership was rumbling when a new Congress took over in 1976. Said one veteran House Republican, "Rhodes is inclined to be more retiring than Ford or Halleck, and the party needs a more aggressive and articulate spokesman for Republican alternatives." Young House Republicans felt the leadership lacked aggressiveness, but they decided to await the 1978 election to consider overthrowing Rhodes and others.

That election put Newt Gingrich of Georgia in the House, and he and several other freshmen let it be known they, too, were displeased with the Republican leadership. "I couldn't help suspecting that many of the machinations were self-seeking . . . so they could begin to climb to the top faster than would ordinarily be possible for freshmen," Rhodes said in his autobiography.

Rhodes felt he could win, "but much blood would be shed and there would be divisions in the party." He wanted no part of a "bifurcated leadership" and began thinking harder about retiring. Finally he decided that he would run for reelection and, if the Republicans gained control of the House, he would be Speaker, but if the Republicans were not in the majority, he would not seek another term as minority leader. The latter is what happened, and he was succeeded by Bob Michel of Illinois. He accepted a seat on the Rules Committee, but it was to be his last term. He was succeeded by a retired military hero, John McCain. When McCain ran for the Senate, Rhodes's son Jay won his father's old seat.

When Rhodes announced he would retire, political columnist John Kolbe of the *Phoenix Gazette* wrote on January 25, 1982, that he had "brought a steadiness, a quiet but unflagging confidence to the conduct of the politician's craft. Every bill he wrote, argument he ameliorated, issue he debated, or task he undertook, he touched with a consummate sense of decency."

After he left office, he went to work for a prestigious law firm with offices around the world. He became international president of his college fraternity, Beta Theta Pi, for three years and served on the boards of the Taft Institution and the Hoover Institution for War, Revolution and Peace.

Rhodes considered one last fling at politics in 1987, when Governor Evan Mecham was threatened with recall. Friends approached Rhodes about succeeding Mecham, but before the election could be held, Mecham was impeached and Secretary of State Rose Mofford, a Democrat, took over.

"I was terribly disappointed, as were the people who were supporting me," Rhodes said. "I felt that, at my age [seventy-one], I would not run for a full four-year term as governor, but that in the two years and seven months remaining in the Mecham term I could do a lot of things for the state that were difficult politically but needed to be done."

Rhodes is now retired and lives in Mesa, Arizona.

Bibliography

Chapter 1—McCain

Altman, Lawrence K. "Release of McCain's Medical Records Provides Unusually Broad Psychological Profile." *New York Times,* December 6, 1999.

Gibbs, Nancy. "Primary Questions." *Time,* November 15, 1999.

Landler, Mark. "McCain, in Vietnam, Finds the Past Isn't Really Past." *New York Times,* April 27, 2000.

Leonard, Mary. "Why McCain Changed on Use of Fetal Tissue." *Boston Globe,* February 13, 2000.

Lewis, Michael. "My Friend the Loose Cannon." *Time,* February 14, 2000.

McCain, John. "What I've Learned." *Esquire,* July 2000.

——, with Mark Salter. *Faith of My Fathers.* New York: Random House, 1999.

"McCain Returns to Vietnam." *Tucson Citizen,* April 25, 2000.

"McCain's Press Appeal—More Than Doughnuts." Reuters, February 9, 2000.

Mitchell, Alison. "Temperament Issue Poses Test for McCain." *New York Times,* November 5, 1999.

O'Connor, Anne-Marie. "Despite His Maverick Appeal, McCain's Home Base May Need Bracing." *Los Angeles Times,* November 23, 1999.

Page, Clarence. "New Hampshire and the Making of a Media Darling." *Chicago Tribune,* February 6, 2000.

Timberg, Robert. *John McCain: An American Odyssey.* New York: Touchstone, 1995.

Von Drehle, David. "Arizona: The Losers' State." *The Gazette* (Montreal), March 11, 2000.

"White Tornado." *Newsweek,* November 15, 2000.

Wilson, Steve. "Sure, McCain Gets Good Media, but There's a Reason." *Arizona Republic,* February 5, 2000.

Chapter 2—Greenway

Aikman, Duncan. "Mrs. Greenway Charts Her Own Course." *New York Times,* April 21, 1935.

Brophy, Blake. "Tucson's Arizona Inn: The Continuum of Style." *Journal of Arizona History,* Autumn 1983.

Cook, James E. "Pioneer Women: Arizonans Blazed Trails in Holding Office." *Arizona Republic,* March 8, 1994.

"Death Claims Isabella King." *Arizona Daily Star,* December 19, 1963.

Martin, Chris. "Isabella Greenway: Influential Arizona Congresswoman." *Northwest Explorer,* September 6, 2000.

Morrison, Betty. "Isabella Greenway: Influential Arizona Congresswoman." Master's thesis, Arizona State University, 1977.

Chapter 3—Stewart Udall

Amos, Wayne. "Inside Interior's Udall." *Arizona Republic,* June 4, 1967.

Carson, Donald W., and James W. Johnson. *Mo: The Life and Times of Morris K. Udall.* Tucson: University of Arizona Press, 2001.

Conconi, Charles. "An Interview with Stewart Udall." *EQM,* May 1973.

Gibson, Daniel. "Vignette: Stewart Udall." *Santa Fean Magazine,* November 1992.

Haederle, Michael. "Unmasking the Myth." *Los Angeles Times,* August 9, 1994.

Manning, Robert. "Secretary of Things in General." *Saturday Evening Post,* May 20, 1961.

Steer, Peter. Oral history, Special Collections, University of Arizona Library, October 24, 1996.

Udall, Stewart L. "Human Values and Hometown Snapshots: Early Days in St. Johns." *American West* magazine, May–June 1982.

——. Interview with author and Donald W. Carson. Santa Fe, New Mexico, July 18, 1998.

Chapter 4—Mecham

Bellus, Ronald J. *Mecham: Silence Cannot Be Misquoted.* Phoenix: Laurent's, 1988.

Decker, Cathleen. "Arizona's Chaotic Politics." *Los Angeles Times,* April 24, 1990.

Jenkins, Sammy S. Sr. *Mecham: Arizona's Fighting Governor.* Albuquerque, N.M.: All States Publishing, 1988.

Mecham, Evan. *Wrongful Impeachment.* Self-published, 1998.

Myers, John L., ed. *The Arizona Governors: 1912–1999.* Phoenix: Heritage Publishers, 1989.

Nichols, Dave. *Nichols' Worth of Ev.* Phoenix: Nichols Books, 1988.

Rosenstiel, Thomas B. "Mecham: An Outsider on the Inside." *Los Angeles Times,* April 21, 1987.

Siegel, Mark. *The World According to Evan Mecham.* Phoenix: Blue Sky Press, 1987.

Watkins, Ronald J. *High Crimes and Misdemeanors.* New York: William Morrow, 1990.

Chapter 5—Douglas

Browder, Robert Paul, and Thomas G. Smith. *Independent: A Biography of Lewis W. Douglas.* New York: Knopf, 1986.

Carlson, Raymond. "Presenting: Lewis W. Douglas." *Arizona Highways,* May 1968.

Cosulich, Bernice. "Mr. Douglas of Arizona." *Arizona Highways,* September 1953.

Goff, John S. *Arizona Biographical Dictionary.* Cave Creek, Ariz.: Black Mountain Press, 1983.

Chapter 6—O'Connor

Ayres, B. Drummond Jr. "A Reputation for Excelling: Sandra Day O'Connor." *New York Times,* July 8, 1981.

Holding, Reynolds. "Sitting in Judgment." *San Francisco Chronicle,* October 29, 1995.

Kammer, Jerry. "Justice O'Connor Puts Retirement Rumors to Rest." *Arizona Republic,* May 1, 2001.

Kohn, Howard. "Front and Center." *Los Angeles Times* magazine, April 18, 1993.

Malone, Julia. "New Right Strategy: Let's Drag out O'Connor's Confirmation Hearing." *Christian Science Monitor,* September 3, 1981.

Marquand, Robert. "Sandra Day O'Connor: Conversations with Outstanding Americans." *Christian Science Monitor,* January 28, 1997.

Sandra Day O'Connor, www.supremecourthistory.org/justice/ o'connor/htm.

Sandra Day O'Connor, The Oyez Project, Northwestern University, www.oyez.new.edu/justices.

Silverman, Matt. "Most Gracious: Insights into Justice Sandra Day O'Connor." *Arizona Attorney,* October 2000.

Chapter 7—McFarland

Chanin, Abe, with Mildred Chanin. *This Land, These Voices.* Flagstaff, Ariz.: Northland Press, 1977.

McFarland, Ernest. *Mac: The Autobiography of Ernest W. McFarland.* Self-published, 1979.

Myers, John L., ed. *The Arizona Governors: 1912–1990.* Phoenix: Heritage Publishers, 1989.

Shadegg, Stephen C. *Arizona Politics: The Struggle to End One-Party Rule.* Tempe: Arizona State University, 1986.

Chapter 8—Hunt

Kleindienst, Richard. *Justice: The Memoirs of an Attorney General.* Ottawa, Ill.: Jameson Books, 1985.

Lockwood, Frank C. *Arizona Characters.* Los Angeles: Times-Mirror Press, 1928.

Myers, John L., ed. *Arizona Civilization.* Phoenix: Hoover Publishing, 1968.

———. *The Arizona Governors: 1912–1990.* Phoenix: Heritage Publishers, 1989.

Shadegg, Stephen C. *Arizona Politics: The Struggle to End One-Party Rule.* Tempe: Arizona State University, 1986.

Chapter 9—Goldwater

Barnes, Bart. "Goldwater, GOP Hero, Dies." *Washington Post,* May 30, 1998.

Chanin, Abe, with Mildred Chanin. *This Land, These Voices.* Flagstaff, Ariz.: Northland Press, 1977.

Cooke, Alistair. *Memories of the Great & the Good.* New York: Arcade Publishing, 1999.

Edwards, Lee. *Goldwater: The Man Who Made a Revolution.* Washington, D.C.: Regnery Publishing, 1995.

Gerson, Michael J. "Mr. Right: Barry Goldwater Created, yet Stood Apart, from Modern Conservatism." *U.S. News,* August 8, 1998.

Goldberg, Robert Alan. *Barry Goldwater.* New Haven, Conn.: Yale University Press, 1995.

Goldwater, Barry, with Jack Casserly. *Goldwater.* New York: Doubleday, 1988.

"The Goldwaters: An Arizona Story and a Jewish History as Well." *Southwest Jewish History,* Spring 1993, Southwest Jewish Archives, University of Arizona.

Greenberg, David. "Goldwater's Glitter." *American Prospect,* May–June 1996.

Iverson, Peter. *Barry Goldwater: Native Arizonan.* Norman: University of Oklahoma Press, 1997.

——. "This Old Mountain Is Worth the Fight." *Journal of Arizona History,* Spring 1997.

Lehrer, Jim. *The NewsHour,* Public Broadcasting Station, May 29, 1998.

Murphy, Michael. "Conservative Pioneer Became an Outcast." *Arizona Republic,* May 31, 1998.

Nachtigal, Jerry. "Barry Goldwater Dead at 89." Associated Press, May 29, 1998.

Chapter 10—Mofford

Carson, Susan R., and Mary K. Reinhart. "Mofford Rules out Run for Governor." *Arizona Daily Star,* January 19, 1990.

Kelly, Rita Mae. *Women and the Arizona Political Process.* Lanham, Md.: University Press of America, 1988.

Myers, John L., ed. *The Arizona Governors: 1912–1990.* Phoenix: Heritage Publishers, 1989.

Pittman, David, and Joseph Garcia. "Legislators Call Mofford a 'Calming Influence' on Arizona." *Tucson Citizen,* January 19, 1990.

Chapter 11—Steiger

Bailey, Eileen. "Sam Steiger: What's Fare Is Fare." *Arizona Republic,* May 18, 1994.

Barks, Cindy. " 'The Tiger' Grabs Politics by the Tail." *Daily Courier* (Prescott, Ariz.), December 12, 1999.

Decker, Cathleen. "Arizona's Chaotic Politics." *Los Angeles Times,* April 24, 1990.

Duncan, Mark. " 'Kill the Lawyers,' Unless You Need One." *Daily Courier* (Prescott, Ariz.), December 12, 1999.

"Famous Arizona Feuds." *Arizona Republic,* July 21, 1995.

Fitzpatrick, Tom. "What Makes Sammy Run?" *Phoenix New Times,* March 7, 1990.

Hostetler, Darrin. "Nibble on the Governor Wanna-bes and See If Any Stay Down." *Phoenix New Times,* September 5, 1990.

Murray, Joe. " 'Typical' Arizonan from New York Says State Is a Haven for Nation's Losers." *Atlanta Constitution,* April 21, 1993.

Shadegg, Stephen C. *Arizona Politics: The Struggle to End One-Party Rule.* Tempe: Arizona State University, 1986.

Shaffer, Mark. "Steiger Returns To Political Spotlight: Elected as Prescott Mayor." *Arizona Republic,* September 9, 1999.

Steiger, Sam, and Don Dedera. *Kill the Lawyers!* Payson, Ariz.: Prickly Pear Press, 1990.

Walker, Dave. "Steiger: The Last Angry Oracle of Old Arizona." *Arizona Republic,* July 4, 1999.

Watkins, Ronald J. *High Crimes and Misdemeanors.* New York: William Morrow, 1990.

Chapter 12—Babbitt

Babbitt, Bruce. "Where the Rivers Flow . . . Again." Speech before the Ecological Society of America, Baltimore, Maryland, August 1998. Reprinted in *Headwaters,* Summer 1998.

"Babbitt Seen as State's Prodigal Son." Cox News Service, printed in *Arizona Daily Star,* July 23, 1995.

Brownstein, Ronald. "Babbitt's New Politics." *National Journal,* March 9, 1985.

Goff, John S. *Arizona Biographical Dictionary.* Cave Creek, Ariz.: Cave Creek Press, 1983.

Haurwitz, Ralph K.M. "It's Babbitt vs. GOP on the Environment." *Austin (Texas) American-Statesman,* September 2, 1995.

Johnson, David. "For Babbitt, a Wearying Exoneration." *New York Times,* October 15, 1999.

Kenworthy, Tom. "Babbitt Viewed as Practical, Able." *Washington Post,* December 25, 1992.

———. "Pragmatic Critic Is Set to Be Interior's Next Landlord." *Washington Post,* January 19, 1993.

Lindsey, Robert. "Babbitt of Arizona: Practitioner of Neoliberalism." *New York Times,* March 17, 1985.

Margolis, Jon. "The Scandal Culture Reaches Bruce Babbitt." *High Country News,* February 2, 1998.

Marston, Ed. "Interior View: Bruce Babbitt Took the Real West to Washington." *High Country News,* February 12, 2001.

———. "It's deja vu yet again, says Bruce Babbitt." *High Country News,* May 1, 1995.

Myers, John L., ed. *The Arizona Governors: 1912–1990.* Phoenix: Heritage Publishers, 1989.

National Center for Public Policy Research, www.national center.org/dos32babbitt.html.

Paulson, Michael. "Babbitt Shows Abrasive Outlook—by a Dam Site." *Seattle Post-Intelligencer,* July 5, 1999.

Riley, Michael. "Babbitt Thrives in Crossfire of Industry, Environmentalists." *High Country News,* August 22, 1994.

St. Clair, Jeffrey. "Babbitt Is No Stegner or Abbey." *High Country News,* September 6, 1993.

Shadegg, Stephen C. *Arizona Politics: The Struggle to End One-Party Rule.* Tempe: Arizona State University, 1986.

Udall, Stewart L. "Friendship Transcended Politics." *Arizona Republic,* May 30, 1998.

Von Drehle, David. "Arizona: The Losers' State." *The Gazette* (Montreal), March 11, 2000.

Chapter 13—Ashurst

Goff, John S. *Arizona Biographical Dictionary.* Cave Creek, Ariz.: Black Mountain Press, 1983.

Goldwater, Barry. *Speeches of Henry Fountain Ashurst of Arizona.* Phoenix: Arizona-Messenger Printing Co., 1953.

Johnston, Alva. "The Dean of Inconsistency." *Saturday Evening Post,* December 25, 1937.

Smith, Mrs. White Mountain. "Old Bill Ashurst's Kid." *Desert Magazine,* June 1940.

Sparks, George F., ed. *A Many-Colored Toga: The Diary of Henry Fountain Ashurst.* Tucson: University of Arizona Press, 1962.

——. "The Speaking of Henry Fountain Ashurst." Ph.D. diss., University of Arizona Library, Special Collections, 1952.

Tolby, Quentin. "Courtroom Oratory Put Judge to Test." *Arizona Republic,* June 28, 1995.

Udall, Morris K., Bob Neuman, and Randy Udall. *Too Funny to Be President.* New York: Henry Holt, 1998.

Chapter 14—Rehnquist

Greenhouse, Linda. "The Justices: The Rehnquist Fact: Abiding Conservatism, Past and Present." *New York Times,* June 19, 1986.

Innes, Stephanie. "Protesters Turn out for Rehnquist." *Arizona Daily Star,* February 3, 2001.

Margasak, Larry. "Rehnquist Hopes Vote Role Will Not Recur." Associated Press, printed in *Arizona Daily Star,* January 1, 2001.

"Profile: William Rehnquist." CNN.com, December 23, 1998.

Roddy, Dennis. "Just Our Bill." *Pittsburgh Post-Gazette,* December 2, 2000.

Sinatra, Amy. "Presiding Over the Senate." ABCNEWS.com, October 6, 1998.

Wagner, Dave. "Rehnquist Tactics in '62 Vote Were Probed." *Arizona Republic,* January 10, 1999.

William H. Rehnquist, www.biography.com.
William H. Rehnquist, www.supremecourthistory.org/.

Chapter 15—Mo Udall

Carson, Donald W., and James W. Johnson. *Mo: The Life and Times of Morris K. Udall.* Tucson: University of Arizona Press, 2001.

Lipske, Michael. "On Capitol Hill, He Provided an Eloquent Voice for Conservation." *National Wildlife,* April–May 2000.

Udall, Morris K., Randy Udall, and Bob Neuman. *Too Funny to be President.* New York: Henry Holt, 1988.

Chapter 16—Lockwood

Chanin, Abe, with Mildred Chanin. *This Land, These Voices.* Flagstaff, Ariz.: Northland Press, 1977.

Elm, Adelaide. Interview with Virginia Hash. Evo DeConcini Oral History Project: Arizona Legal History, March 9, 1987, University of Arizona Law Library.

Jacobs, Thomas A., and Nancy L. Matte. "Justice Was a Lady: A Biography of the Public Life of Lorna E. Lockwood." Unpublished paper written for Arizona Historical Society, University of Arizona Law Library, 1985.

Quantz, David M. "A Legal Biography of Lorna E. Lockwood." Unpublished, University of Arizona Law Library, n.d.

———. "Lorna Lockwood: A Dynamic Woman in Changing Times." Unpublished, University of Arizona Law Library, February 14, 1986.

Chapter 17—Hayden

August, Jack L. *Vision in the Desert: Carl Hayden and Hydropolitics in the American Southwest.* Fort Worth: Texas A&M Press, 1999.

Cohen, Jerry. "Carl Hayden—Man of History and Few Words." *Los Angeles Times,* April 18, 1971.

Rice, Ross. *Carl Hayden: Builder of the American West.* Lanham, Pa.: University Press of America, 1994.

———. *Carl T. Hayden, 1877–1972,* www.asu.edu/lib/archives/azbio/hayden.html.

Shadegg, Stephen C. *Arizona Politics: The Struggle to End One-Party Rule.* Tempe: Arizona State University, 1986.

Thimmesch, Nick. "Carl: After 57 years, the Senate's Last Frontiersman Goes Home." *Los Angeles Times,* January 5, 1969.

Tributes to Honorable Carl Hayden, Senator from Arizona, to Commemorate the Occasion of His Fiftieth Anniversary of Congressional Service, February 19, 1962. Washington: United States Government Printing Office, 1962.

Udall, Morris K. *Congressman's Report,* March 13, 1972.

Chapter 18—Castro

Calderon, Ernest. Interview with Raul H. Castro, July 7 and July 10, 1999. Arizona Bar Foundation Oral History Project, Arizona Historical Society.

Chanin, Abe, with Mildred Chanin. *This Land, These Voices.* Flagstaff, Ariz.: Northland Press, 1977.

Myers, John L., ed. *The Arizona Governors: 1912–1990.* Phoenix: Heritage Publishers, 1989.

Shadegg, Stephen C. *Arizona Politics: The Struggle to End One-Party Rule.* Tempe: Arizona State University, 1986.

Wynn, Bernie. "One Man's Opinion." *Arizona Republic,* October 16, 1970.

Chapter 19—Symington

Fischer, Howard. "Symington, Funds Reach $2M Deal," *Arizona Daily Star,* September 14, 2001.

Fischer, Howard, and Jon Burstein. "Symington Prevails; U.S. Has Next Move." *Arizona Daily Star,* June 23, 1999.

Flannery, Pat. " 'The Most Elegant Way to End This Saga,' " *Arizona Republic,* January 21, 2001.

———. "Symington Was Ready to Make a Deal." *Arizona Republic,* January 24, 2001.

"Major Events in the Career of Former Gov. Fife Symington." Associated Press, February 16, 2001.

Sherwood, Robbie. "Why a Pardon? Symington Saved Clinton's Life, Story Goes." *Arizona Republic,* January 21, 2001.

Symington, Fife. "Symington, for the Record." *Arizona Republic,*
September 29, 1991.
"Symington Friend Helped Gain Pardon." *Arizona Daily Star,*
February 26, 2001.
Van Biema, David. "Arizona, the Scandal State." *Time,* June 24, 1996.

Chapter 20—Kleindienst

Goldwater, Barry, with Jack Casserly. *Goldwater.* New York:
Doubleday, 1988.
Kleindienst, Richard. *Justice: The Memoirs of an Attorney General.*
Ottawa, Ill.: Jameson Books, 1985.
"Republican Architect: Kleindeinst Was a Major Player in GOP's
Rise Here." *Arizona Republic,* February 6, 2000.
"Richard G. Kleindienst, Watergate Figure, Dies at 76." *Arizona
Daily Star,* February 4, 2000.
"Richard Kleindienst: U.S. Attorney General Brought Down by
Watergate Scandal." *The Guardian,* February 5, 2000.
"Richard Kleindienst, Attorney General During Watergate, Dies."
Washington Post, February 4, 2000.
Shadegg, Stephen C. *Arizona Politics: The Struggle to End One-Party
Rule.* Tempe: Arizona State University, 1986.

Chapter 21—Rhodes

Cohen, Richard E. "House Republicans Under Rhodes—Divided
They Stand and Fret." *National Journal,* October 29, 1977.
Rhodes, John, with Dean Smith. *John Rhodes: 'I Was There.'* Salt Lake
City: Northwest Publishing, 1995.
Shadegg, Stephen C. *Arizona Politics: The Struggle to End One-Party
Rule.* Tempe: Arizona State University, 1986.

Index

chancellor of McGill University, 48; death of, 51; early years, 45–46; education, 46; elected to Arizona House, 46; elected to U.S. House, 46–47; eye injury, 49–50; hero, 44–45; quits over deficit spending, 48; relationship with royal family, 50–51; retires to ranch, 51; selected as budget director, 47; service in army, 46; works in mines, 46

Douglas, Lewis W., Jr., 46
Douglas, Peggy Zinsser, 46
Douglas, Sharman, 46
Douglas, William O., 126
Ducheneaux, Frank, 139
Dukasis, Michael, 106
Dulles, John Foster, 51

Eden, Anthony, 50
Eisenhower, Dwight D., 51, 65, 79, 179
Elizabeth II, Queen of England, 50
Elson, Roy, 83
English, Karan, 5, 24

Fallon, Richard, 128
Falwell, Jerry, 57, 85
Fannin, Paul, 4, 15, 97, 180
Fennimore, Dick, 180
Ferguson, Martha, 19
Ferguson, Robert, 19
Ferguson, Robert, Jr., 19

Ford, Gerald, 56, 93, 185, 188, 190
Fortas, Abe, 148
Frank, John, 147
Frick, Henry Clay, 169
Frick, Henry Clay II, 186
Frohmiller, Ana, 5, 6, 186

Garcia, Jesus, 44–45
Garfield, James A., 137
Garner, John Nance, 47, 48
Gingrich, Newt, 190
Goddard, Sam, 38, 181
Goddard, Terry, 99, 171
Gold, Vic, 82
"Golden Age," 187
Goldwater, Baron, 76
Goldwater, Barry, 3, 4, 7, 8, 10, 14, 32, 34, 35, 37, 51, 57, 64, 65, 66, 67, 71, 104, 106, 108, 113, 126, 134, 140, 153, 155, 157, 169, 178, 179–81, 184–5, 188–9; 1964 presidential race, 81–83; antsypants, 78; best-selling author, 80; Central Arizona Project, 78–79; confronts Nixon, 84; death of, 86; early years, 76; education, 77; elected to Senate, 79; elected to Senate in 1968, 83; health deteriorates, 84–85; liberal leanings, 85–56; love of Arizona, 78; military service, 77; named most admired, 75; opposes Civil Rights Act, 80; re-elected, 80; relationship

Lockwood, Lorna (*continued*)
to Arizona supreme court,
145–6; elected to legislature,
143; elected to superior court,
144; Judge's Prayer, 146; mentor, as, 141; opens law practice, 143; study of law, 142–
143; takes over juvenile court,
144; twice considered for U.S.
Supreme Court, 147–148;
works for father, 143
Long, Huey P., 119

Madison, James, 140
Margaret, Princess, 50, 51
Marshall, General George C., 49
Marshall, George P., 31
Marshall, Thurgood, 60, 128,
148
McArthur, Douglas, 10
McCain, Andy (stepson), 11
McCain, Bridget (daughter), 13
McCain, Carol Shepp (first wife),
11, 13
McCain, Cindy Hensley, 13
McCain, Doug (stepson), 11
McCain, Jack (son), 13
McCain, Jim (son), 13
McCain, John S., Sr. (grandfather), 10
McCain, John S., Jr. (father), 10,
13, 16
McCain, Senator John S. III, 3, 4,
8, 106, 139, 190; attends
Naval Academy, 10–11; early
years, 10; elected to Congress,
13–14; elected to Senate, 14;
embroiled in savings-and-loan
scandal, 14–15; explosion on
Forrestal, 11–12; future in
Senate, 17; introduction to
politics, 13; mentioned as vice
presidential candidate, 15;
nicknames, 9–10; prisoner of
war, 12–13; pyschological
evaluation, 15–16; runs for
president, 16–17; shot down
over Vietnam, 12; visits Vietnam, 13
McCain, Meghan (daughter), 13
McCain, Roberta (mother), 10
McCain, Sidney (daughter), 11
McCarthy, Eugene, 30
McCarthy, Joe, 179
McCormack, John, 136
McCormick, Byron, 162
McFarland, Clare Collins, 62
McFarland, Edna Eveland Smith,
63
McFarland, Ernest, 3, 4, 7, 78–
79, 120, 155, 179–80, 185;
attends Stanford law school,
62; chosen Senate majority
leader, 64; death of, 68; defeated by Goldwater, 64–65;
early years, 62; elected to Arizona Supreme Court, 67; elected governor, 65–66; elected
Pinal County attorney, 62–63;
elected superior court judge,
63; elected to U.S. senate, 63;
G.I. Bill, 61–62, 64; inves-

tigation, 63; loses again to Goldwater, 66–67; McFarland State Park, 68; Miranda decision, 67; motion picture industry, 63–64; opens practice, 62; represents Winnie Ruth Judd, 63; serves in navy, 62; Triple Crown of Politics, 61

McFarland, Jewell, 63

McGovern, George, 30

McGregor, Ruth, 53, 56

McRae, Laura, 143

Mecham, Christine, 37

Mecham, Dennis, 37

Mecham, Eric, 37

Mecham, Evan, 6, 88, 90–91, 92, 98, 99, 104, 155–6, 168, 170, 171, 173, 181–2, 191; cancels King holiday, 41; description of, 36; early years, 36; gaffes, 41; impeached, 42; indicted, 42; loses bid for Arizona House, 37; loses bid for governor, 38; loses bid for governor in 1990, 42; loses bid for U.S. senate, 37; opens auto dealership in Ajo, Arizona, 37; recall begins, 42; removed from office, 42; ridiculed, 36–37; serves in army air corps, 36; starts newspaper, 38; supports from, 36; wins governorship in 1986, 40; writes campaign autobiography, 39; writes *Wrong Impeachment*, 43

Mecham, Florence Lambert, 36

Mecham, Kyle, 37

Mecham, Lance, 37

Mecham, Suzanne, 37

Mecham, Teresa, 37

Meyers, Charles J., 68

Michel, Bob, 190

Minorities in Arizona politics, 5–7

Miranda case, 67

Mitchell, John, 126, 181

Mock, Tonya, 100

Moeur, Benjamin Baker, 73

Mofford, Frances, 89

Mofford, John, 89

Mofford, Rose, 6, 191; becomes governor, 90; description, 90; early career, 89; early years, 89; leaves governor's office, 88–89; on Mecham's removal from office, 91; praised, criticized, 92–93; work ethic, 90

Mofford, T. R. "Lefty," 89

Molera, Jaime, 6

Montgomery, Field Marshal, 44

Moore, Louise, 143

Mormons, 27–28, 36, 73–74

Morrison, Bob, 162

Munds, Frances Willard, 5

Murdock, John, 144, 185, 186–7

Nader, George, 164

Napolitano, Janet, 6

Nimitz, Admiral Chester, 10

Nixon, Richard, 81, 84, 126, 164, 177, 179, 188–9

About the Authors

JAMES W. JOHNSON is a journalism professor at the University of Arizona. He is the co-author of *Mo: The Life and Times of Morris K. Udall* and *One Step from the White House: The Rise and Fall of Senator William F. Knowland.*

DAVID FITZSIMMONS is the political cartoonist for the *Arizona Daily Star* in Tucson.